WRITER
WILLIAM MESSNER-LOEBS

PENCILERS
GEOF ISHERWOOD & MIKE DEODATO JR. WITH LUKE ROSS, OCLAIR ALBERT, FRANK TOSCANO, DANTE BASTIANONI & PINO RINALDI

INKERS
GEOF ISHERWOOD, MIKE DEODATO JR. & DEODATO STUDIOS WITH RENE MICHELETTI, EDDE WAGNER, GRANT NELSON, ALEX JUBRAN, BRAD VANCATA & ANDY LANNING

COLORISTS
MARIE JAVINS, JOHN KALISZ & MALIBU WITH FRANK LOPEZ

LETTERERS
MICHAEL HIGGINS & JON BABCOCK

ASSISTANT EDITORS
MATT IDELSON & POLLY WATSON

EDITORS
RALPH MACCHIO & BOBBIE CHASE WITH MARK GRUENWALD

FRONT COVER ARTISTS
MIKE DEODATO JR. & TOM CHU

BACK COVER ARTISTS
MIKE DEODATO JR. & TOM SMITH

COLLECTION EDITOR
MARK D. BEAZLEY

ASSISTANT EDITORS
NELSON RIBEIRO & ALEX STARBUCK

EDITOR, SPECIAL PROJECTS
JENNIFER GRÜNWALD

SENIOR EDITOR, SPECIAL PROJECTS
JEFF YOUNGQUIST

RESEARCH & RECAP TEXT
DANA PERKINS

LAYOUT
JEPH YORK

PRODUCTION
COLORTEK & RYAN DEVALL

SVP OF PRINT & DIGITAL PUBLISHING SALES
DAVID GABRIEL

EDITOR IN CHIEF
AXEL ALONSO

CHIEF CREATIVE OFFICER
JOE QUESADA

PUBLISHER
DAN BUCKLEY

EXECUTIVE PRODUCER
ALAN FINE

THOR: SUNLIGHT & SHADOWS. Contains material originally published in magazine form as THOR #495 and #497-502. First printing 2013. ISBN# 978-0-7851-6267-4. Published by MARVEL WORLDWIDE, INC., a subsidiary of MARVEL ENTERTAINMENT, LLC. OFFICE OF PUBLICATION: 135 West 50th Street, New York, NY 10020. **Printed in the U.S.A.** ALAN FINE, EVP - Office of the President, Marvel Worldwide, Inc. and EVP & CMO Marvel Characters B.V.; DAN BUCKLEY, Publisher & President - Print, Animation & Digital Divisions; JOE QUESADA, Chief Creative Officer; TOM BREVOORT, SVP of Publishing; DAVID BOGART, SVP of Operations & Procurement, Publishing; C.B. CEBULSKI, SVP of Creator & Content Development; DAVID GABRIEL, SVP of Print & Digital Publishing Sales; JIM O'KEEFE, VP of Operations & Logistics; DAN CARR, Executive Director of Publishing Technology; SUSAN CRESPI, Editorial Operations Manager; ALEX MORALES, Publishing Operations Manager; STAN LEE, Chairman Emeritus. For information regarding advertising in Marvel Comics or on Marvel.com, please contact Niza Disla, Director of Marvel Partnerships, at ndisla@marvel.com. For Marvel subscription inquiries, please call 800-217-9158. **Manufactured between 9/20/2013 and 10/28/2013 by R.R. DONNELLEY, INC., SALEM, VA, USA.**

10 9 8 7 6 5 4 3 2 1

MARVEL

UNIVERSE

ISSUE 495

FEBRUARY 1996

STILL $1.50

APPROVED BY THE COMICS CODE AUTHORITY

THOR

BY MESSNER-LOEBS & ISHERWOOD

GRINDBERG AFTER THE "KING" '95

MORTAL CHAMPION!

Stan Lee presents
IN MORTAL GUISE
NEW YORK THE CITY IS SO QUIET, GLEAMING IN THE DARKNESS. IT LOOKS SO MUCH NICER THAN IT WOULD DISSOLVING INTO PRIMAL OOZE, OR OVERRUN BY THOUSANDS OF "NEW MEN", HUNGRY FOR BLOOD!
TRUE.
GEOFF ISHERWOOD - - guest artist
MICHAEL HIGGINS - - letterer
MALIBU - - computer color
MARIE JAVINS & FRANK LOPEZ - - colorists
RALPH MACCHIO - - editor
and
MARK GRUENWALD - - editor in chief
welcome aboard new writer
BILL MESSNER-LOEBS

THIS IS YET ANOTHER TIME WHEN THIS WORLD OWES YOU A DEBT, MY THOR... NO, ALL OF EXISTENCE OWES YOU. AND YET YOU GET NOTHING.
IT WAS PRICE'S MISCALCULATION. I DID NOTHING REALLY. STILL...

STILL? WHAT ARE YOU THINKING, O LORD OF THUNDERS?
THAT PRICE WAS MORTAL. HOW D HE GAIN THE KNOWLEDGE TO M THE SCALDINGS FROM ASH AN OLD RADIO PARTS? HOW WAS ABLE TO FIND AND TORMENT T WORLD TREE?

WOULD I SEEM HORRIBLY SHALLOW IF I TOLD YOU I DON'T CARE? STEP OUT ON THE BALCONY, LORD. YOUR REWARD AWAITS.

MISTRESS? WHEN WILL YOU RETURN?
WHEN I WILL. KEEP EVERYTHING IN READINESS FOR ME. AND NO SLACKING.
THE WARM WIND CARESSES MY BARE SKIN BENEATH THE ROBE. I SMELL THE SCENT OF STRAWBERRIES IN HER HAIR. EACH BREATH FILLS ME WITH EXCITEMENT.
HER NAME IS AMORA, AND SHE IS KNOWN AS THE ENCHANTRESS. SHE WAS ONE OF MY GREATEST ENEMIES, BUT SHE IS NO LONGER.

EVERYTHING HAS CHANGED.

ALL MY LONG LIFE I HAVE LIVED AT THE RIGHT HAND OF THE ALL-FATHER, AS RESPONSIBLE AS HE FOR THE HEALTH OF ASGARD AND THE FATE OF THE WORLD. MOMENTS LIKE THESE, WHEN I CAN LIVE FOR MYSELF ARE **RARE** AND **SWEET**.
SEE YOU BROUGHT OUR HAMMER, MY LOVE. WHY?
BECAUSE I ALWAYS BRING IT, I SUPPOSE. IT IS AS MUCH A PART OF ME AS MY **LEG**.
O YOU SEE THEM DOWN ERE, AMORA? POOR PEOPLE, CH PEOPLE... LIVING THEIR VES AND BEING HAPPY. THEY ILL NEVER KNOW HOW **CLOSE** E ALL CAME. **THAT** IS EWARD ENOUGH FOR ME.
I WOULD HAVE MADE THEM **BEAT** THEMSELVES WITH CHAINS AND **GASH** THEMSELVES WITH COPPER KNIVES IN GRATITUDE!
WHICH EXPLAINS WHY THAT **AVENGERS MEMBERSHIP** FOR ME HAS ALWAYS BEEN SO ELUSIVE.
AND NOW I THINK WE CAN MOVE ON TO **STAGE TWO** OF YOUR REWARD...

THE HOME OF VICTOR PRAZNIKI, THE LEADER OF THE MACHINISTS' UNION, A VERY WEALTHY MAN.

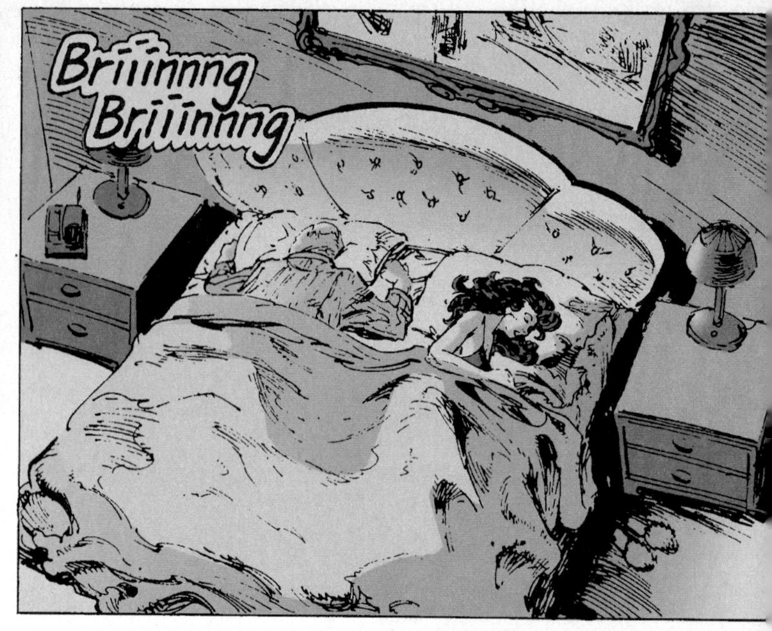
Briiinnng
Briiinnng

Briiinng

SILVIE...? SILVIE, YOU GO' THAT?
Briiinng

'LO...?
LISTEN, PRAZNIKI, THIS IS YOUR ONLY WARNING. WE KNOW YOU GOT IT. CROSS US AGAIN AND YOU'RE DEAD!

WHAT...? WAIT!
WE KNOW WHERE YOUR WIFE SHOPS AND WHERE YOUR DAUGHTER GOES TO SCHOOL. IT'D BE A REAL SHAME IF SOMEBODY MESSED THEM UP. A REAL SHAME.

KLIK

MMMMMMM...

GOOD MORNING.
INDEED. THE SUN IS BEAUTIFUL THROUGH THE TREES...

TREES?
GRASS? WHERE ARE WE?
IT'S A PARK, AND THERE ARE BUILDINGS THROUGH THE TREES.
CENTRAL PARK. BUT HOW DID WE GET HERE? WHERE IS THE SPHERE?

MY POWERS OF ENCHANTMENT-- *GONE!*

HOW IS THIS POSSIBLE, THOR?

YOUR **HAMMER**
SEE IF IT STILL
RETAINS ITS OW
ASGARDIAN
MAGIC.
LET US SEE IF WE ARE BOTH SIMILARLY BEREFT.

ONE BLOW RETURNS THE HAMMER AND ME TO OUR PREVIOUS GODLY FORMS. **TWO** BLOWS CALL THE LIGHTNING... THREE THE **DIRE STORM**.
THUD

NOTHING.

EY, BILLBO. DIG THE FREAKS!
IT'S AS THOUGH EVERY DROP OF MAGIC HAS BEEN LEECHED OUT OF THE WORLD OVER NIGHT.
MAYBE WE SHOULD TEACH THEM A LESSON, SO'S THEY WON'T ACT LIKE STUPID FREAKS IN OUR TERRITORY.
SRRNK
YOU ARE RIGHT, EVEN THE SIMPLEST OF MY CHARMS ARE GONE.
ET'S START HERE! NOBODY UGHT TO HAVE THIS MUCH AIR! IT AIN'T NATURAL M GONNA TAKE IT FOR A BELT!
IT'S AS THOUGH SOMETHING WERE MISSING.
SOMETHING IMPORTANT.
FUMP
UHHMMP!
WUMP
YES. I KNOW WHAT YOU MEAN.

HEY, YOU FREAKIN' FREAGS! YOU BROGG MY DOZE!
THERE IS A STILLNESS, ALMOST A VACUUM OF THE SPIRIT.

YOU DINK I DON'T GOTTA GUN! I GOTTA GUN!
AS IF EVERY MAGICAL ESSENCE HAD WITHDRAWN FROM THE EARTH...

...LEAVING US ALONE...
THWAK

...AND DEFENSE-LESS!
AHHHHHH!

WELL, THAT WAS FUN!
BUT WHAT DO WE DO NOW?
Eeeeep!
Ahhhhh!

WE HAVE TO RETURN TO YOUR APARTMENT, WHICH IS DUE WEST FROM HERE, I THINK. ONCE ON THE STREET, WE CAN GET OUR BEARINGS.

YES. MAYBE MY SLAVES HAVE HEARD SOMETHING THAT WILL EXPLAIN THIS.
IT'S ABOUT FIFTY BLOCKS FROM HERE! BUT, THANK BORI, THE WEATHER IS MILD.
LOOK! HALF-NAKED LUNATICS IN THE MIDDLE OF WINTER!

THE REACTION OF NEW YORK'S HUMANS TO LIGHTLY-CLAD BODIES HAS ALWAYS AMAZED ME.
PARK
IN ASGARD, THE POPULACE TROOPS EN MASSE TO THE SPRING EVERY MORNING TO BATHE. I'VE ALWAYS KNOWN WHAT MY FRIENDS AND ENEMIES LOOK LIKE IN THEIR SKIN.

YET HERE, PEOPLE ARE ALWAYS AMAZED BY IT, AS THOUGH THEY HAD NEVER SEEN ANYONE UNDRESSED! AS I SAY, UNFATHOMABLE!

LOOK AT THAT, JIMMY.
WHAT?

THAT CROWD. THERE'S A COUPLE O' NUTS DRESSED IN ROBES!
SO WHAT, LEGS? THIS IS NEW YORK! THERE'S ALWAYS KINDA PROMOTION GOING ON!

DO WE EVEN KNOW WHERE TO FIND THE GIRL?
YEAH. I GOTTA CALL BEFORE WE LEFT. SHE'S MEETING SOMEBODY AT THE CONSTRUCTION SITE AT 53RD. AND CAMPBELL.

BUT WE'RE GONNA MEET HER FIRST, HUH, JIMMY?
AND TEACH HER A LESSON?

YEAH.

T LAST THE LONG
ALK IS OVER AND
E LEFT A SMALL
IRONG OUTSIDE AS
E TOOK THE PRIVATE
EVATOR TO THE
ENTHOUSE, ONLY
TO FIND...

ASH

THE DOOR'S OPEN!
IS THIS THEIR IDEA OF SECURITY? SOMEONE WILL...
NOOOO! THE APARTMENT HAS BEEN STRIPPED! MY COLLECTIONS! MY ANTIQUES! MY ARTWORKS!
HUNDREDS OF THOUSANDS OF DOLLARS! A MILLENNIUM OF COLLECTING! WHAT HAPPENED HERE? WAS IT A RAID? WERE ALL MY SLAVES KILLED? ARE THEY COMING BACK?

PERHAPS THIS WILL SAY...

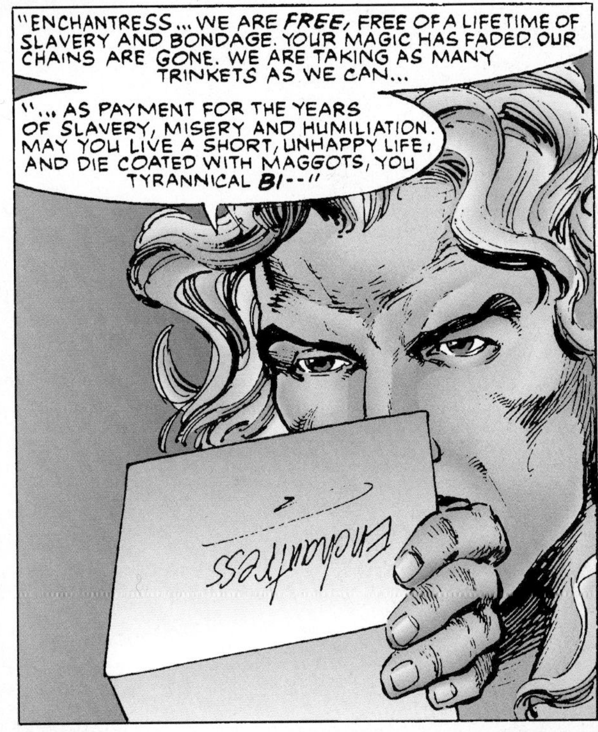
"ENCHANTRESS... WE ARE FREE, FREE OF A LIFETIME OF SLAVERY AND BONDAGE. YOUR MAGIC HAS FADED. OUR CHAINS ARE GONE. WE ARE TAKING AS MANY TRINKETS AS WE CAN...
"... AS PAYMENT FOR THE YEARS OF SLAVERY, MISERY AND HUMILIATION. MAY YOU LIVE A SHORT, UNHAPPY LIFE, AND DIE COATED WITH MAGGOTS, YOU TYRANNICAL BI--"
Enchantress

'D SAY THEY'RE OT COMING ACK.
AARRGGH!

ONE OF AMORA'S MOST ADMIRABLE QUALITIES IS HER FLEXIBILITY UNDER STRESS... ONCE SHE'S HAD A CHANCE TO VENT, OF COURSE.
TRINKETS, EH? I'LL HAVE THEIR BLACKENED BONES CARVED INTO TRINKETS! I'LL DRINK FROM JEWEL ENCRUSTED GOBLETS MADE FROM THEIR SKULLS!

THEY EVEN TOOK THE REFRIGERA- TOR! AND THE OVEN AND... THOR, ARE YOU LISTENING T ME?!

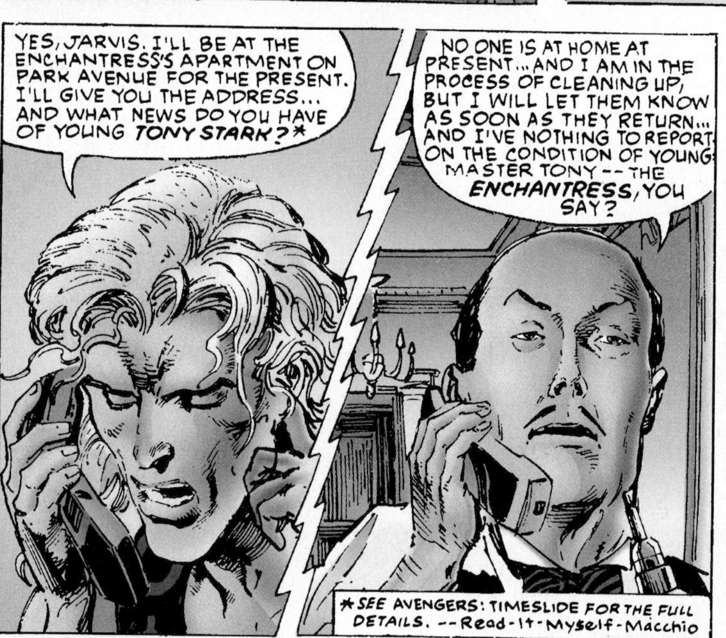
YES, JARVIS. I'LL BE AT THE ENCHANTRESS'S APARTMENT ON PARK AVENUE FOR THE PRESENT. I'LL GIVE YOU THE ADDRESS... AND WHAT NEWS DO YOU HAVE OF YOUNG TONY STARK?*
NO ONE IS AT HOME AT PRESENT... AND I AM IN THE PROCESS OF CLEANING UP, BUT I WILL LET THEM KNOW AS SOON AS THEY RETURN... AND I'VE NOTHING TO REPORT ON THE CONDITION OF YOUNG MASTER TONY -- THE ENCHANTRESS, YOU SAY?
*SEE AVENGERS: TIMESLIDE FOR THE FULL DETAILS. --Read-It-Myself-Macchio

HI, NEIGHBOR!
I'M PHILIP FLEMING, TH MANAGER HERE AT TH ASH. WE HAVEN'T MET BUT I'M A BIG FAN OF YOUR LADY FRIEN THE SUPERNATURAL AND ALL THAT.
Tap
Tap

I COULDN'T HELP BUT NOTICE ALL THE STUFF SHE MOVED OUT OF HERE TODAY... SHE IS PLANNING ON SETTLING PAST DUE RENT BEFORE SHE LEAVES, ISN'T SHE?

Um... WE WON'T BE MOVING, I THINK.
FINE, THAT'S FINE. HERE'S YOUR MAIL, MR. VISION. LOOKS LIKE A LOT OF BILLS. Um... SHE DOESN'T SIGN AUTO- GRAPHS, DOES SHE? HER BEING AN AVENGER AND ALL? IT'S NOT FOR ME...

INALLY, MR. FLEMING WENT AWAY.
THEY LEFT US THIS TURKEY AT LEAST, IF WE FIGURE OUT A WAY TO ROAST IT. WHAT ARE YOU DOING?
LOOKING UP CONSTRUCTION COMPANIES. IN MY MORTAL IDENTITY I USED TO WORK HIGH STEEL.

SOON I'LL FIGURE OUT A CHARM TO GET MY WEALTH BACK. THERE'S NO NEED...
I LIKE TO WORK AND ANYWAY THE RENT ON THIS PLACE WILL REQUIRE TWO INCOMES...

AND MOVE THAT BIRD! THE VATER'S COLD!
COMPLAIN, COMPLAIN.

IF ONLY WE HAD A WAY TO ROAST IT. BUT SHORT OF RIPPING UP THE FLOOR BOARDS TO MAKE A PYRE...

YOU MIGHT ASK THE BUILDING MANAGER. HE'S QUITE A FAN OF YOURS, EX-CEPT HE THINKS YOU'RE THE SCARLET WITCH!

HA! HA! HA! HA! HA!
THERE IS SOMETHING QUITE LOVABLE ABOUT A WOMAN WHO CAN LAUGH IN THE FACE OF SUCH A SITUATION.

I FINALLY DECIDED TO WANDER THROUGH A FEW CONSTRUCTION SITES. I'D GOTTEN HIRED THAT WAY BEFORE. BUT THE ECONOMY WAS WORSE NOW. NO ONE VISITED THESE SITES UNLESS...

...THEY WERE IN REAL TROUBLE.
I REMEMBER HOW USED TO COME TO PLACES LIKE THIS AND WAIT FOR DAD IF ONLY...

HELLO, ANNIE. YOUR POP'S IN TROUBLE, WHICH MEANS YOU'RE IN TROUBLE.

IT'S SO EASY FOR A PRETTY GIRL LIKE YOU TO HAVE AN ACCIDENT... BANG-BANG!

WHO ARE YOU? LET GO OF ME, YOU BA--

VATCH YOUR @%#! ANGUAGE, LITTLE GIRL. YOU CAN GET URT A LOT OR NLY A LITTLE...

HEY! THIS ONE NEEDS A LESSON, JIMMY!

THERE WERE AT LEAST TWO CARS AND EIGHT MEN, AND I WAS TOO CLOSE NOW TO TRY FOR SURPRISE.
LET HER GO!

HEY, PAL, THIS S A PRIVATE PARTY. MIND YOUR OWN BUSINESS OR...
HE WAS YOUNG AND NERVOUS. I COULD SMELL IT ON HIM. AND HE LET ME GET TOO CLOSE BEFORE DRAWING HIS WEAPON.

FOOL.
WHAK

I HAD TO MOVE QUICKLY AND FORCE THE BATTLE. IN A MELEE, THEY WOULD HESITATE TO USE THEIR MOST POWERFUL WEAPONS.
OKAY, BOZO. YOU JUST USED UP ALL YOUR LUCK. NOW GET ON YOUR KNEES...
THEY HAD NOT THOUGHT YET TO USE THE GIRL AS A SHIELD. AS LONG AS THEY UNDERESTIMATED ME, WE WERE SAFE...
TO THINK HE WOULD ASK SUCH OF AN ASGARDIAN...

WUK
KRAT

PRAK

BRAP

C'MON, NEF! THERE'S NOBODY BE- HIND HIM! WE CAN SPRAY--

MY BREATHING HAD BECOME RAGGED. I COULD FEEL MY HEART SHUDDER. THEY WEREN'T VERY GOOD, BUT THEY WERE WELL-ARMED AND TRIGGER-HAPPY. AND I WAS MORTAL.

I HAD TO END THIS NOW!

GET HIM!
HOLD HIM!

YEEOOOWWWCCHH!

COME ON! SHE'S GETTING AWAY!

GRAB 'ER!
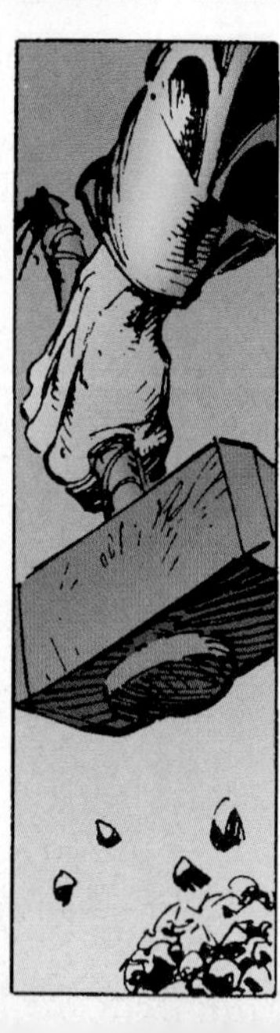

HELP!
HOLY--! HE'S TRYING TO CATCH! SHOOT HIM!

THUD
BLAM

YAAAAA!

RRRRRRR

OHMIGOD! RUN!

KRASH
WHUAAMMPP

HIS IS
XCITING.
NYTHING
SHOULD
NOW
BOUT?
I HONESTLY HAVE NO IDEA. THEY WERE ACTING... BAD. I STOPPED THEM.

SOUNDS RIGHT TO ME.

WE STOPPED AT THE APARTMENT. YOUR... LADY FRIEND TOLD US WHERE YOU'D GONE.
WE'RE TRYING TO PULL THE AVENGERS TOGETHER AGAIN. YOU WERE THERE AT THE BEGINNING... WOULD YOU WANT TO RE-JOIN US?

WITH ALL MY HEART. BUT... I AM A GOD NO LONGER. I HAVE ONLY A MORTAL'S STRENGTH AND A MORTAL'S SKILL. I WOULD NOT ENDANGER THE REST OF YOU.

I SEE. AND YOU DID ALL THIS WITHOUT ANY POWERS?

YOU'LL DO.
MARVEL
END

When the villainous Zodiac group, led by the mysterious Libra, raised an impenetrable force field around Manhattan that deactivated all electricity, Captain America found himself pursued by the Zodiac's agents, whose lethal laser cannons were the only working technology in the city. Hoping to recruit Thor, the only other Avenger he knew to be trapped inside the field, Cap led the Zodiac agents to the Enchantress' uptown apartment — but upon arrival he was shocked to learn that Thor and the Enchantress had lost their godly powers.

With the Enchantress' help, Thor and Cap defeated the attackers, and Thor theorized that the Asgardians' power loss was due to a side effect of the damage inflicted upon the Norse world-tree Yggdrasil days before by the lunatic scientist Price. Learning that Libra was teleporting his agents into the city from a mobile transportal device based in an abandoned subway station, Thor and Cap headed there on foot, but found the darkened streets choked with Zodiac agents and panicked, rioting civilians. Though Thor was still adjusting to being mortal, he held his own — and when Cap was injured, Thor battled through the troops using both his hammer and Cap's indestructible shield.

The two Avengers arrived at the subway station, but were overwhelmed by additional troops arriving through the portal. However, Tony Stark arrived and turned the tide, though it nearly drained his armored gauntlets' failing power — and the three stole the Zodiac skimmer craft that housed the portal and fled for the force field's edge. Using the portal to open a small hole in the field, the heroes let in their teammates Giant-Man, Wasp, Quicksilver and Deathcry. Quicksilver searched the city at super-speed, locating the Zodiac's force-field generator — and while the other Avengers battled Libra, Giant-Man destroyed the generator, dissipating the field and restoring Manhattan's power.

Soon after this battle, the gamma-mutated Omnibus, mentally influenced by the Hulk's old foe the Leader, committed terrorist attacks against several worldwide landmarks. When the Hulk tried to thwart Omnibus' plans, the villain engineered a distraction: he secretly restored Thor's godly might, and orchestrated a massive battle between the two heroes! The brawl was interrupted when the US military nuked the battle site, but Thor's restored powers remain… though for how long, he does not know.

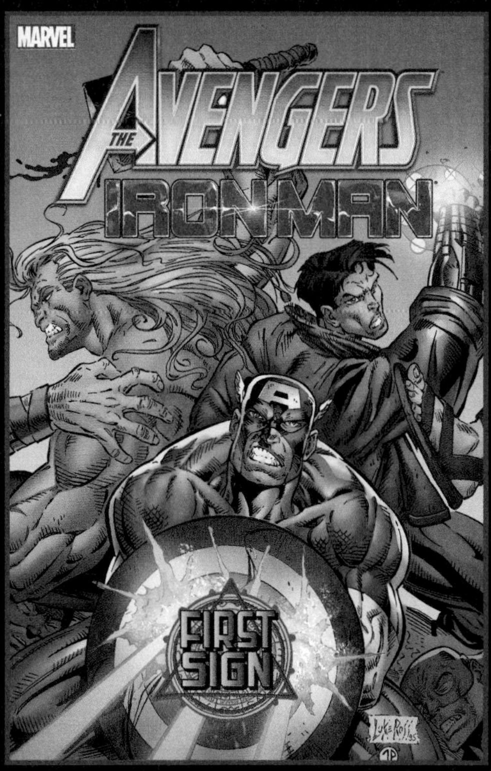

MARVEL
UNIVERSE
APPROVED BY THE COMICS CODE AUTHORITY
THOR
STILL $1.50
...FATHER?!

CHANGE.
I LOOK DOWN UPON NEW YORK, MY ADOPTED HOME CITY, AND THINK ABOUT THE CHANGES THAT HAVE BROUGHT ME HERE.
EXILED FROM MY NATIVE ASGARD AND ESTRANGED AT LAST FROM MY FATHER, ODIN, I HAVE FOUND MYSELF MAROONED AMONG MORTALS. EVEN MY GREAT STRENGTH AND THE POWER OF MY URU HAMMER HAVE BEEN STRIPPED FROM ME.
THEN, A DAY AGO, IN THE MIDST OF BATTLE AGAINST AN ENRAGED HULK, ALL MY POWERS RETURNED, THROUGH THE MACHINATIONS OF THE STRANGE, TWISTED BEING KNOWN AS THE LEADER.
I HAVE NOT EVEN THE SLIGHTEST NOTION OF HOW LONG THIS ARTIFICIAL RESTORATION OF MY GIFTS WILL LAST, BUT I MEAN TO MAKE THE MOST OF IT! NEVER DID I REALIZE HOW I LOVED THE STRENGTH AND POWER AND FLIGHT OF A GOD UNTIL I LOST THEM!
THOR MUST DIE
I LOOK DOWN UPON THE CITY-- A VAST SPRAWLING BEHEMOTH, FILLED TO OVERFLOWING WITH LIFE NO LESS CHAOTIC THAN MY OWN-- AND I AM CONTENT.
THEN I NOTICE THAT SOMEONE HAS WRITTEN, IN FLAMING LETTERS EACH AS LARGE AS A SMALL HORSE-- "THOR MUST DIE!"
Ah, NEW YORK. AS JANE FOSTER USED TO SAY, "YOU HAVE TO LOVE IT."
STAN LEE PRESENTS: SOME MORE THOR!
Wm. MESSNER-LOEBS wrote it... aided by LUKE ROSS, OCLAIR ALBERT & FRANK TOSCANO (All of whom drew it...) RENE MICHELETTI, EDDIE WAGNER, GRANT NELSON & ALEX JUBRAN inked it, while BABCOCK lettered it, KALISZ colored it, MALIBU COMPUTERIZED it, and RALPH MACCHIO, MARK GRUENWALD & BIG BOB HARRAS edited it (all done simultaneously) (No--REALLY!)

AN INSULT-SLASH-WARNING, SPELLED OUT IN FLAMING FLOWER POTS. THIS TRAP, AND IT MUST BE A TRAP, AT LEAST HAS THE VIRTUE OF NOVELTY.
NOW, THE ONLY QUESTION IS, WHO...?
SO, YOU'VE COME TO DIE!
BY THE SACRED ASH!
MEN CALL ME RAZORFIST, BUT YOU CAN JUST CALL ME THE LAST THING YOU'LL EVER SEE, THUNDER-DUD!
AND DON'T PRETEND YOU'RE NOT TERRIFIED, 'CAUSE YOU ARE!

THUNDER-BOY, HERE, DOESN'T HAVE ANY POWER! FOR THE LAST MONTH I BEEN SPYING ON HIM, HE'S BEEN FIGHTING JUST LIKE A REG-ULAR GUY.
HE DOESN'T LOOK TERRIFIED TO ME, MARCO.
THAT'S 'CAUSE YOU DON'T KNOW HIS SECRET! AND CALL ME RAZORFIST, REMEM-BER, ESTELLE?
IT MUST'VE HAPPENED WHEN HE GOT SICK, REMEMBER? WE HEARD IT ON THE POLICE SCANNER. THAT WAS WHEN I REALIZED I COULD USE HIM FOR MY PLAN.
YOU MEAN THE PLAN WHERE YOU DEFEAT ONE OF THE AVENGERS AND TAKE HIS PLACE ON THE TEAM 'CAUSE THE REST OF THEM ARE SO INTIMIDATED BY YOU?
Yeah. THEY'LL THINK I'M A BAD GUY, AT FIRST, 'CAUSE I KILLED THEIR FRIEND AND ALL. BUT THEN THEY'LL LET ME REFORM AND-- BINGO!--
--I'M AVENGERS MATERIAL!
AND THOR IS PERFECT! HE'S VULNERABLE TO ALL THE GADGETS I DESIGNED FOR US, BUT HE'S STILL GOT THE REP, SO HIS DOWNFALL WILL BE MUCHO IMPRESSIVE!
WATCH THIS!
I THINK I'M ABOUT TO DO A BAD THING...

KRRAKADOOOM!

MARCO!
MARCO! ARE YOU OKAY?
unhh.
HE... HE GOT POWERS, ESTELLE!
MARCO, YOU IDIOT. OF COURSE HE GOT POWERS!

HE FLEW DOWN HERE AFTER HE SAW YOUR SIGN...
THE ONLY WAY HE COULDA SEEN IT WAS IF HE HAD POWERS!
WHAT WERE YOU THINKING?
I FIGURED IT WAS AN ILLUSION... YOU KNOW, LIKE A HOLO-GRAM.
IT DOESN'T MATTER! I'LL HIT 'IM HARD NOW, WHEN HE DOESN'T EXPECT IT.

THROOB
THROOB
WUD!

Oh, Geez. NOW YOU MADE HIM MAD!

KRAKOW
MAN. RALPH ONLY LOANED US HIS PENT-HOUSE FOR THE WEEK-END! HE'S GONNA KILL US!
KEEP AWAY, YOU BULLY! KEEP AWAY OR MY VORTEX-STAFF WILL...
WILL...
...uh...
HOW COME YOU COULD STOP MY STAFF WITH YOUR BARE HANDS?
I'M A GOD.
Oh, Yeah.

SO, YOU WANT TO FLY, DO YOU?
LET GO OF THE SPIRAL, YOU--THAT COSTUME IS RENTED!

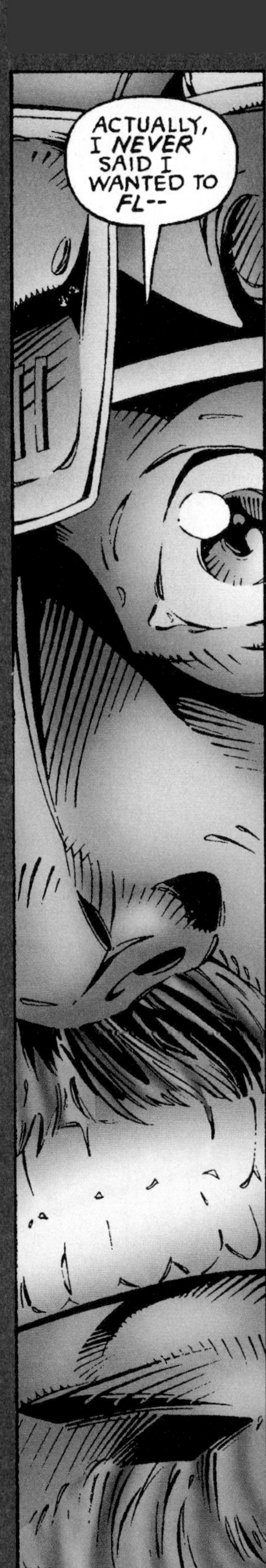
ACTUALLY, I NEVER SAID I WANTED TO FL--

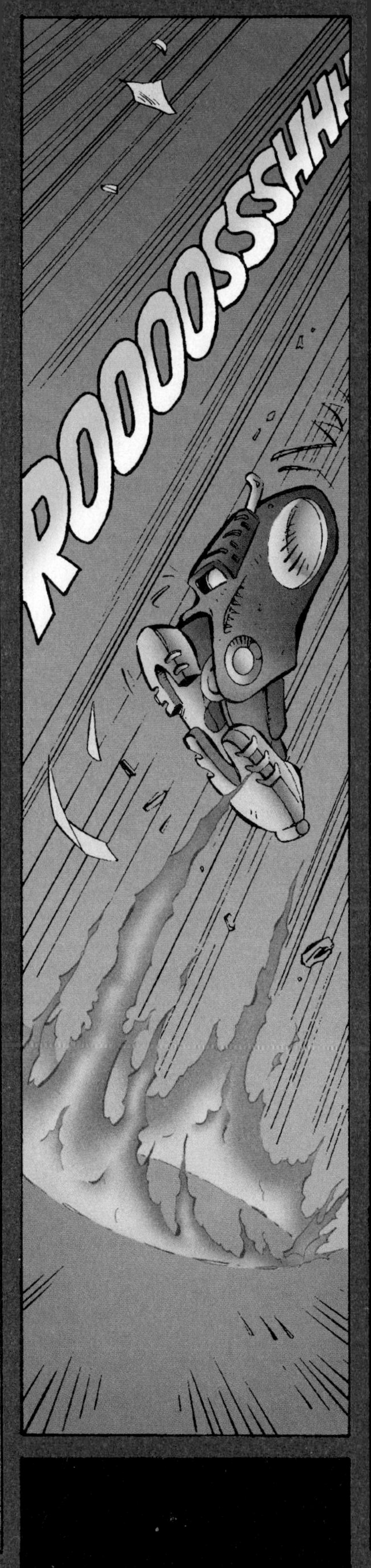
ROOOOSSSHHH

AAAAAAAHHHHHHHHHHHH

uhhhh!
THIS IS THE WORST, MARCO! I THOUGHT IT WAS BAD WHEN YOU AND YOUR IDIOT FRIENDS WRECKED MY CORVETTE, BUT THAT WAS NOTHING!
SO YOU WISH TO BE AN AVENGER, AYE? LET ME SEE IF THERE IS A SITUATION IN THE CITY WORTHY TO TEST YOUR METTLE!
Ah...!
"JUST THE THING... A DRUG SWEEP HAS GONE WRONG IN CENTRAL PARK. TWO GANGS, ENEMIES ORDINARILY, HAVE JOINED IN BATTLING THE POLICE.
"WOEFULLY SHORT-HANDED, THE OFFICERS IN THE TWO PATROL CARS ARE OVERWHELMED. HOSTAGES ARE TAKEN.
"NOTE THE WOUNDED OFFICER. HER FELLOWS ARE HELPLESS TO AID HER. WITHOUT ASSISTANCE, THIS PARK WILL BECOME A SITE OF ESCALATING TRAGEDY."

FOR-TUNATELY, YOU TWO ARE IDEALLY TRAINED AND ARMED TO SUBDUE THE MIS-CREANTS!
WE-- WE ARE?
OF COURSE YOU ARE! BE BRAVE!
ST-STAY BACK... OR FACE THE WRATH OF RAZORFIST! I SAID STAY BACK! STAY...
YAAAAA!
THERE'S HUNDREDS OF THEM! THEY'LL KILL US!
INDEED? I THOUGHT YOU WERE MAKING EXCELLENT PROGRESS.
PERHAPS I CAN PROVIDE A DISTRACTION...

...FOR I AM LORD OF THE WINDS...
"...AND THE STORM!"
POLICE

"THUNDER AND LIGHTNING ARE MY HUNTING DOGS...
BRRAKKAADOOOM!
"...THE RAIN IS MY WHIP...
"...AND WHEN I MUST, I RIDE A GREAT AND TERRIBLE STEED...
NYPD

"... THE EARTHQUAKE!"
POLICE
FRAAAKKGGRAAANNDDDTT

"NOTHING MORTAL CAN STAND BEFORE IT."
I'M OFFICER GAUNT, KIM GAUNT. YOU JUST SAVED MY BLINKING LIFE, SO WE OUGHT TO BE ACQUAINTED.
WAY-COOL, THUNDER-GUY!
AND I LOVE YOUR CROWD-CONTROL TECHNIQUE!
THIS IS DARCIA. SHE GOT CAUGHT IN THE CROSS-FIRE WHEN THIS CRACK-SWEEP WENT SOUR.
HELLO, DARCIA.
...DUNNO WHAT HAPPENED. THE HAWKS AND THE ARYAN DREAM WOULD RATHER BITE IT THAN TEAM UP!
HEY, LOOK OVER THERE! IT'S Mr. SUPER HERO WHO WRECKED OUR BROTHERS!

YOU THINK WE'RE GONNA LET YOU AND THIS WITCH-COP WALK AWAY FROM HERE, AVENGER?
THAT WOULD BE THE INTELLIGENT MOVE, YES.
NOT WHEN I GOT THREE HOSTAGES NOW! I CAN STILL UNITE ALL THE GANGS IN NEW YORK!
SKIN
I DON'T BELIEVE THEY'VE LEARNED ANY-THING YET!
TIME FOR ANOTHER LESSON, Huh?
THE FIRST ONE WAS IN CIVICS! THIS ONE WILL BE IN HUBRIS!

friiksshh

HEY, THE HAMMER DIDN'T WORK!
HE'S JUST A REGULAR GUY NOW!
THIS IS GONNA BE FUN!
Uh-Oh.
I DON'T SUPPOSE THIS IS ALL PART OF YOUR CLEVER PLAN? WHERE THE CAVALRY COMES RIDING OVER THE HILL JUST ABOUT N--?
VILLAINS! TASTE THE BITTER, FULSOME VENGEANCE THAT IS RAZORFIST!
CHARLES LOVES DI

WUP!
THAK!
IN ALL MY DREAMS, THE LAST THING I EXPECTED WAS THAT MARCO WOULD ACTUALLY BE GOOD AT THIS!
FWAAP!
EAT BLASTER, SCUMBAG!
NOBODY TOUCHES A BROTHER AVENGER WHILE RAZORFIST IS ON THE SCENE!
YAAAAAA! I'M A T-T-T-TOP!
AND NOBODY BOTHERS MARCO SAN ANTONIO WHILE ESTELLE GEIS IS ON THE JOB!
CODE-NAMES, ESTELLE, USE THE CODE-NAMES...
SKUUNCH!!

SO WHAT IF MY MEN ARE ALL DOWN? SO WHAT? I STILL GOT THIS STUPE, AND I STILL GOT YOU!
MIGHT AS WELL PUT THAT HAMMER DOWN!
I SAID PUT IT DOWN! WE BOTH KNOW IT'S OUTTA BATTERIES OR WHATEVER! IT'S JUST A HUNK OF IRON NOW!
UNLESS YOU REALLY CAN THROW ANOTHER LIGHTNING BOLT! YEAH, GO AHEAD! FRY ME ALIVE!
I DARE YOU! FRY ME! GO ON, FRY M--
KRAKKA-THOOOM!!
IT'S A GIFT.

THOR...?
I DON'T *BELIEVE* IT! IT'S NOT *POSSIBLE!*
THAT OLD MAN OVER THERE... HE LOOKS LIKE... BUT HE *CAN'T* BE...
...HE...
...IS...
ALL-FATHER?

THOR?
THOR, CAN YOU TELL US IF THIS RIOT WAS PART OF SOME LARGER PLAN BY Dr. DOOM OR MAYBE THE ABSORBING MAN?
DID YOU REALLY CAUSE AN EARTH-QUAKE?
THOR?
THOR?
ARE YOU HERE AS AN AVENGERS REPRESEN-TATIVE?
IS IT TRUE YOU'VE REGAINED YOUR POWERS?
ARE YOU A CLONE?
PLEASE...
PLEASE! I HAVE TO SEE...
GONE.

SILVIE? YOU GOT THAT SANDWICH YET?
CNN
AND IN THE NEWS TODAY...
ERE YOU
O, VICTOR.
GG SALAD
ITH JUST
SPRINKLE
F TABASCO,
HE WAY
OU LIKE
IT.
I'M GOING TO THE COFFEE GROUNDS FOR A WHILE, DADDY...
...LATE-BREAKING STORY...
LIKE THAT YOU'RE GOING? I DON'T THINK SO. IT'S DANGEROUS WALKING THE STREETS LIKE A STRUMPET!
Oh, DADDY! IT'S NOT GONNA KILL M--
BRRRAAAATTKKRSSHH
...LIVE...

...WHERE JUST MINUTES AGO A DRUG RIOT WAS STOPPED COLD...
LOUSY, NO-GOOD... ANNIE!
ANNIE?! SPEAK TO US! WHERE ARE YOU SHOT?
I'M ALL RIGHT, MOTHER. I JUST GOT CUT BY THE GLASS!
...MINOR EARTH TREMOR IN MANHATTAN! AND IT ALL WORKED OUT, THANKS TO...
THIS IS THE SECOND TIME THOSE SLEAZEBALLS HAVE TRIED SOMETHING. I GOTTA BUY ME SOME PROTECTION...
...I GOTTA...
...I GOTTA BUY HIM!
...THE MIGHTY THOR!
"...I GOTTA BUY HIM!"
NEED WE SAY IT? TO BE CONTINUED!

Thor house ad by Mike Deodato Jr.

ONCE I WAGED GLORIOUS WAR AS A GOD AMONGST MEN. BUT HOW MUCH GREATER THE HONOR TO FIGHT AS A MAN AMONGST GODS?
THOR
MARVEL COMICS
Putting the Character Back in Comics.
TM & © 1996 Marvel Characters, Inc. All rights reserved.

MARVEL COMICS
M
THOR
MAY '96 498
APPROVED BY THE COMICS CODE AUTHORITY
THOR

"THEY SAY IT'S ACCURSED...!"
Stan Lee Presents Thor in
LIFE PRESERVATION
Wm. MESSNER-LOEBS: WRITER MIKE DEODATO, Jr.: ARTIST, Pgs. 1-11
DANTE BASTIANONI: PENCILS, Pgs. 12-16 PINO RINALDI: PENCILS, Pgs. 17-22
BRAD VANCATA: INKS, PAGES 12-16 ANDY LANNING: INKS, PAGES 17-22
J. BABCOCK: LETTERER MARIE JAVINS: COLORIST MALIBU: SEPARATIONS
RALPH MACCHIO & BOBBIE CHASE: EDITORS BOB HARRAS: CHIEF EDITOR

THE SWORD WAS CALLED RAVEN'S EYE. IT HAS A BLACK DIAMOND IN THE HILT THE SIZE OF A MAN'S FIST.
IT WAS SUPPOSEDLY STOLEN FROM THE NORSE GOD, VOTAN, AT THE BEGINNING OF TIME BY A FROST GIANT WHO LOST IT GAMBLING TO THE FIRST OF A SUCCESSION OF HUMAN REAVER KINGS...
...ALL OF WHOM DIED VIOLENTLY.
SUPPOSEDLY, IT WAS PART OF THE TEMPLARS' LOOT. THEN THEY WERE SLAUGHTERED AND IT MOVED EAST INTO RUSSIA. IT WAS IN THE ROMANOV'S BEDROOM ...UNTIL THE REVOLUTION.
IT BECAME PART OF A SECRET DISPLAY AT THE HERMITAGE. THEN, SOME TIME DURING THE EIGHTIES, IT WAS STOLEN, AND PASSED INTO THE HANDS OF AN INDUSTRIAL CARTEL...
...WHO, IN TURN, GAVE IT TO ME AS A THANK YOU.
ANOTHER OF MY FATHER'S TOYS COME BACK TO HAUNT ME.
A "THANK YOU"...?
IT WAS THE EIGHTIES. AND I DIDN'T MAKE A FUSS WHEN MY UNION INVESTED ITS PENSION FUND IN JUNK BONDS.
AND THERE WERE A COUPLE OF NOT-SO-GOOD CONTRACTS I MANAGED TO GET APPROVED...
...YOU KNOW. IT WAS THE EIGHTIES!

NOW, SOMEBODY WANTS THE SWORD, AND SINCE IT DOESN'T OFFICIALLY EXIST IN THIS COUNTRY, I CAN'T GO TO THE COPS.
AND YOU WANT US TO WHAT, EXACTLY? PROTECT THE SWORD ...OR YOUR FAMILY?
YAWWNN
PROTECT US, OF COURSE.
VIC, HONEY, I DON'T SEE WHY YOU JUST COULDN'T HIRE THE X-MEN!
LIKE YOU REALLY HAVE A VOTE HERE, SIL-VIA! THIS IS FAMILY BUSINESS!
I CAN SAY WHAT I LIKE, ANNIE!
I'M YOUR FATHER'S WIFE! YOU SHOULD SHOW SOME RESPECT!
DON'T TELL ME WHAT TO DO! YOU'RE NOT MY MOTHER!
NOW, GIRLS....!
WE'RE ALL UNDER STRESS SINCE THESE ATTACKS.
THOR, YOU RESCUED ANNIE FROM BEING KIDNAPPED.
SINCE THEN, WE WERE ALL NEARLY KILLED IN A DRIVE-BY SHOOTING. THESE PEOPLE ARE GETTING SERIOUS!
I'VE GOT THE SWORD IN A SAFE PLACE FOR NOW, AND I'M NEGOTIATING WITH A MUSEUM TO TAKE IT OFF MY HANDS. BUT I NEED MY FAMILY PROTECTED.
THIS CITY IS STUFFED WITH SUPER HEROES! BUT THEY CAN'T GIVE ME 24-HOUR SERVICE. THAT'S WHY I NEED YOU!

I'M SENDING MY WIFE AND DAUGHTER TO A SECURE HOUSE OUTSIDE THE CITY TILL THE SWORD IS GONE. I WANT YOU TO PROTECT THEM, JUST LIKE YOU SAVED MY LITTLE PRINCESS.
I WANT TO STAY WITH YOU, DADDY!
I NEED YOU TO BE SAFE, PUMPKIN! AND WITH THOR HERE, THE BULLETPROOF LIMO AND A COUPLE OF THE BOYS TO GUARD YOU, I CAN FINALLY RELAX.

OF COURSE I WILL HELP YOU, Mr. PRAZNIKI. AND WE CERTAINLY HAVE NO DESIRE TO EXPLOIT THE DANGER YOUR FAMILY IS IN. PAYING OUR EXPENSES WILL BE MORE THAN SUFFICIENT.
AMORA WILL WORK OUT THE DETAILS, RIGHT, MY LOVE?

SLAM
NOW THAT THE MORALITY SQUAD HAS LEFT, WE CAN ACTUALLY BEGIN TO NEGOTIATE...

F.L.A.
HELLO, HOME BASE, THIS IS SHUTTLE ONE. WE SHOULD LAND IN ABOUT TWENTY MINUTES.

WELL, I DON'T SEE WHY WE CAN'T STOP SOMEPLACE AND SHOP!
ARE YOU ENJOYING THE BIG ADVENTURE YET, THUNDER GOD?

LOOKS LIKE WE MAY HAVE TO STOP ANYWAY, MA'AM! THE TRAFFIC'S BLOCKED SOLID UP AHEAD.

HEY, YOU!
GET BACK IN THAT CAR! WHADAYA THINK THIS IS, A NATIONAL PA--?

OH, IT'S YOU, THOR! DON'T MIND ME. ALWAYS GLAD FOR AVENGERS' HELP! SOME JACKASS CAUSED AN EARTHQUAKE HERE YESTERDAY. THIS WHOLE STREET HAS TO BE RENOVATED.
KIM...?
I BET IT WAS THAT HULK...

OFFICER GAUNT!
THOR?

I WANTED TO TALK WITH YOU. YOU DISAPPEARED RIGHT AFTER STARTING THAT *EARTHQUAKE.*
Umm... Yes. I NEEDED TO TALK TO YOU, TOO.

DURING THE BATTLE YESTERDAY, I GLIMPSED AN OLD HOMELESS MAN. HE HAD A FULL WHITE BEARD.
I NEED TO FIND THAT MAN.

THERE *IS* A GUY WHO STAY AROUND HER CALLED WA HE USUALL SQUATS IN THAT ALLEY.

WHAT'D HE DO? TEAM UP WITH DOCTOR DOOM?
NO, NOTHING LIKE THAT. I JUST NEED TO *TALK* WITH HIM.
Well, I CAN ASK AROUND, BUT... WHAT'S THAT?
THADLTHADLTHADLTHADLTHADLTHAD
HELICOPTER...?

BRAKA
BRAKA
BRAKA
BRAKA
BRAKA
BRAKA
GET BACK!

SPRRRAATTTCCKKKKK
RATTATRATTABRA
TTABRATTABRA
NO, IT'S NOT!
UHHHHNNN!
SPAK
SPAK
THOR...! THE 'COPTER'S COMING BACK!!
RATTABRATTABR
KRNCH!

DRAATTK!
RARRAM!
THROOOM!
Geez.

THAK!
TWUD!

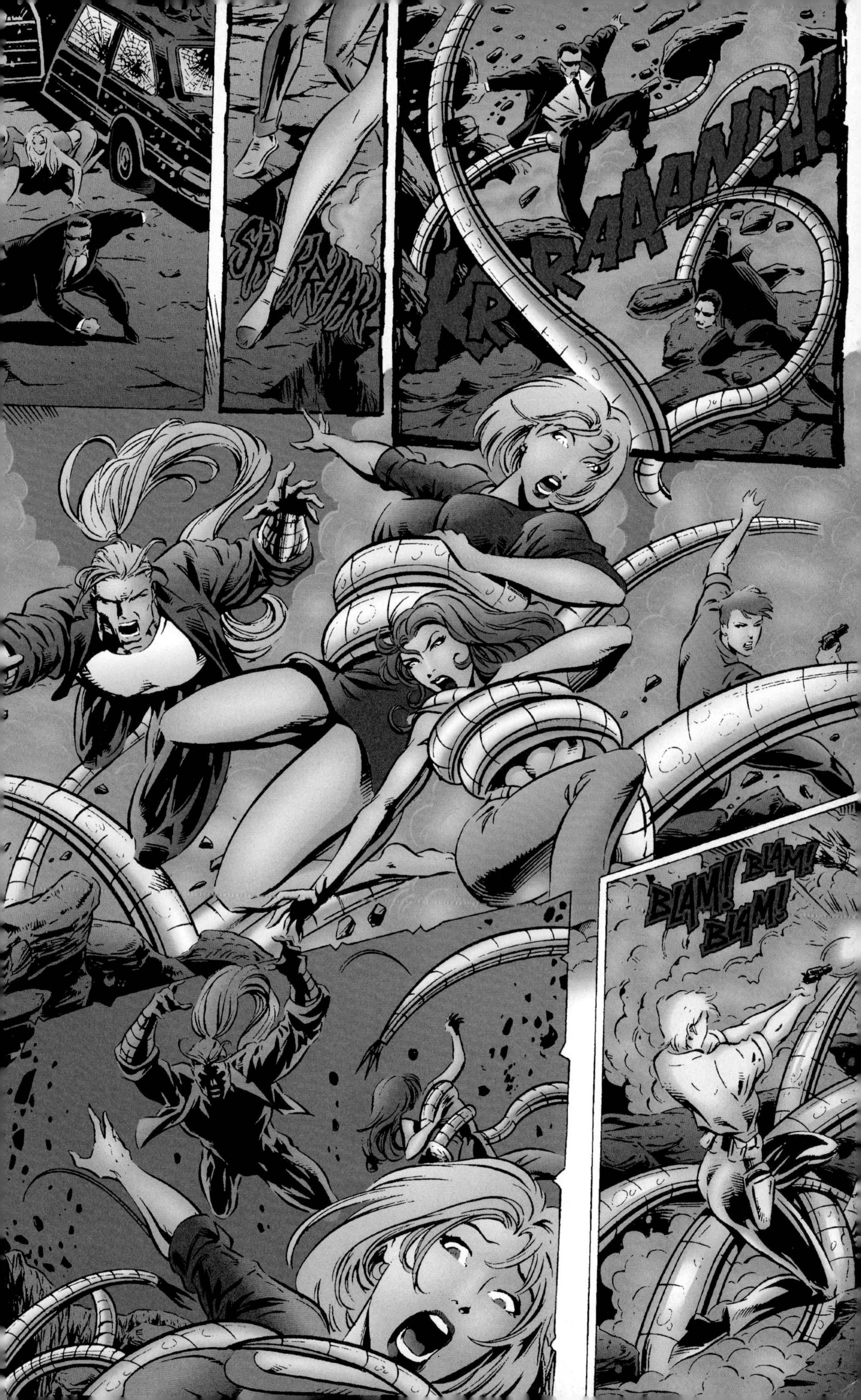
KRRAAAANCH!
BLAM! BLAM!
BLAM! BLAM!

Hah? NOISES?
BATTLE SOUNDS. GOOD SOUNDS...
AND VOICES. I KNOW VOICES
THOR...?
KRIIIGHH

Man. THOSE DINGUSES SHOOK US OFF LIKE WE WE'RE NOTHING!
ANY IDEA WHERE THEY WENT?
Uuhhh...
NO. AND I CAN'T HEAR ANYTHING, EITHER. NOT EVEN THE GRINDING OF MACHINERY.
THIS IS A DIRE AMOUNT OF EFFORT FOR ANYONE TO EXPEND...
...NO MATTER HOW VALUABLE THE SWORD!
MY GUN IS IN THIS MESS SOMEPLACE.
YOU SAY THIS IS ALL OVER A SWORD?
INDEED. SUPPOSEDLY ONE OF MY FATHER'S. AND YET I'VE NEVER HEARD OF IT. HE WAS ALWAYS FULL OF SURP--
SPPOORRRTSSHH!
'LO.

BY BIFROST'S GATE! FATHER! IT IS YOU!
FOUND IT!
VOICES... SOUNDS LIKE MY SON... HAD A SON ONCE... HE WAS A GOOD SON, TOO...
...LIKED HIM... BUT THEN, HE WAS BAD... OR SOMETHING...
...CAN'T REMEMBER...
...YOU GOTTA DRINK?
ODIN, WHAT ARE YOU SAYING? I'M YOUR SON!
YES, HE WAS A GOOD BOY... DEAD NOW. EVER'BODY DEAD NOW... ASGARD DEAD... BROTHERS DEAD 'LONG TIME AGO. DID I SAY I KILLED MY SON...?

DEAD AS 'DOORNAIL. I KILLED HIM. CAME TO ME FOR HELP AN' I SLAMMED THE DOOR IN HIS FACE... BOOM! SO HE DIED!

LISTEN TO ME! MAKE SENSE! I'M YOUR SON!
DEAD... DEAD... ALL DEAD!
FATHER... HOW DID YOU GET TO MIDGARD? HOW LONG HAVE YOU BEEN LIKE THIS?
ALL DEAD. ALL. NO ONE B'LIEVES ME!
I TOLD 'EM. F'YEARS I TOLD 'EM I WAS ALL-FATHER... BUT WOULD THEY LISTEN...?
THOR...
SWEET BYE AND BYE... NOBODY LISTENS...
ONE OF THOSE TENTACLES SCRAPED THE WALL HERE... THEY MUST'VE GONE THAT WAY.

--AND THIS WAS THE SCENE AN HOUR AGO WHEN GIANT SQUID-LIKE ARMS CARRIED FOUR PEOPLE--ONE, THE AVENGER **THOR**--INTO THE NETHERWORLD OF THE SEWERS. MORE AS--
CNN
BRIINNGG
BRINNG
HELLO, DADDY? LISTEN, DADDY, DON'T DO ANYTHING HE SAYS--***AHHH!***
YOUR DAUGHTER IS TOO ***BRAVE*** FOR HER OWN GOOD, DEAR SIR. I'M SURE YOU'LL DO EXACTLY AS I ASK...
ZZZZIIIP

OVER HERE, GUYS. THERE'S ANOTHER MARK.
WHAT I WANT TO KNOW IS WHERE SOMEBODY GETS THE POWER TO RUN THOSE GIZMOS! THEY MUST'VE TAPPED THE CITY'S ELECTRICAL GRID.
POWER! I WAS POWER! I WAS BROTHER TO THE STARS!
WHAT GOOD IS IT TO BE A GOD WHEN NOBODY BELIEVES YOU? ANSWER ME THAT, Eh?
ISN'T THERE A LI'L DRINKY AROUN' HERE ANYWHERE?

Y'KNOW, OLD WAD HERE HAS BEEN IN THAT ALLEY AS LONG AS ANYONE REMEMBERS. YEARS... AND YET, ACCORDING TO YOU, A FEW WEEKS AGO HE WAS LORDING IT OVER ASGARD.
HOW...?
Uh-uh. A WIRE...!
THE CEILING!
A WIRE? A TRAP!
RRRRRRUUUMMMMMBLLLLL
IT'S A DEAD-FALL! RUN!
KEEP GOING!
KEEP GOING!

LOOKS LIKE WE'LL BE DOING OUR **BAT** IMITATIONS FROM NOW ON!
Oooff. I'M GLAD ONLY THE **SMALL** PIECES HIT US!

DO YOU SEE A **LIGHT** DOWN THERE?
YES. IT COULD BE A **DOOR**...

...OR IT COULD BE A **TRAP!** BE READY!
RIGHT BEHIND YOU! ONE... TWO...
WHRAM!
...**THREE!**

HULLO, BROTHER. LATE AS USUAL?
UNTIE THE WOMEN, OFFICER. THIS IS LOKI, MY VILE HALF-BROTHER. HE'LL NOT HARM YOU...
NOT SO HASTY, THOR!
YOU SEE, BROTHER-MINE, THIS WHOLE ROOM IS RIGGED WITH EXPLOSIVES.
TOUCH ME AND YOU'LL REGRET IT.
THIS BLADE IS A TALISMAN OF GREAT POWER. WITH IT IN MY GRASP, THERE'S NOTHING...
MY SWORD!

GIMME SWORD!
FATHER, NO!
GOTCHA...

Oh-oh.

MARVEL® COMICS

THOR®

JUNE '96 499

APPROVED BY THE COMICS CODE AUTHORITY

THE WORLD I SEE ABOUT ME IS AS NEW AND STRANGE AS SOME PAPERBACK FANTASY, AND YET IT'S ALL REAL. MY FATHER, ODIN, IS A DRUNKEN BUM, LIVING IN THE FILTHY ALLEYS OF NEW YORK CITY, AND I DON'T EVEN KNOW WHY.
THIS MORNING I DISCOVERED HIM WHILE I WAS TRYING TO PROTECT THE DAUGHTER OF LABOR CZAR VICTOR PRAZNIKI FROM KIDNAPPERS. THEY WANTED THE SWORD RAVENSEYE. JOINING ME IN THIS WAS OFFICER KIM GAUNT OF THE N.Y.P.D.
EVENTUALLY WE ALL CONFRONTED THE KIDNAPPER-- MY EVIL, HALF-BROTHER, LOKI, WHO NOW HAD THE SWORD. WHEN MY FATHER IMPULSIVELY TOUCHED IT, HE, I AND THE THREE WOMEN WERE TRANSPORTED HERE...
...ALTHOUGH WHERE "HERE" IS, I HAVEN'T THE SLIGHTEST IDEA!
Whoo Boy. ARE WE IN TROUBLE NOW!
STAN LEE PRESENTS...
LUDWIG'S CHILDREN
Wm. MESSNER-LOEBS WRITER
MIKE DEODATO, Jr. ARTIST
JON BABCOCK: LETTERER
MARIE JAVINS: COLORIST
MALIBU: SEPARATIONS
BOBBIE CHASE: EDITOR
BOB HARRAS: ALL-FATHER

ALL-FATHER...? WHAT JUST HAPPENED HERE? DID YOU WORK A SPELL WITH THE SWORD?
SWORD?
I TAKE THE SWORD. HE HAS BECOME A BIBULOUS FOOL.
HOPELESS.
I DON'T THINNGG SHO...
DID I TELL YOU 'BOUT MY SHUN...
WHERE ARE WE? WHERE'S MY DAD?
WHERE'S THE SEWERS AND THE GUY WITH THE HORNS?
WHERE ARE MY CLOTHES? I LOOK LIKE A CIMMERIAN HOOKER!
KEEP THE LOOK! YOU CAN LAND YOURSELF ANOTHER RICH HUBBY FOR YOUR COLLECTION!
KEEP YOUR FILTHY MOUTH SHUT, YOU SPOILED LITTLE SLACKER!
WHY? SO YOU CAN HAVE DADDY ALL TO YOURSELF?
THAT'S YOUR PLAN, DARLING! ASK YOUR FANCY THERAPIST WHAT THAT MEANS!

I LOVE YOUR FATHER! AND IF YOU RUIN, THIS FOR ME--!
Hah! ONLY YOUR PLASTIC SURGEON COULD DO THAT, YOU--
LOOK! COMP'NY!
BORI'S SONS! THEY COME IN A RUSH OF LEATHER AND STEEL, SCREAMING FOR BLOOD! WHO ARE THEY?
FOR ALBRECHT!
YOU'RE ALL UNDER ARREST!
RUSH THE MAN AND THE TALL WOMAN! THE OTHERS ARE HELPLESS!
HEY!

TASTE MJOLNIR'S FURY!
FOR THE GOLD!
CRUSH THE OVER-THINGS!
KILL HIM!
DRINK HIS BLOOD!
Arrrgh. I FORGOT MJOLNIR IS NO LONGER ENCHANTED! IT WILL NO LONGER RETURN TO ME!
AND YOU HAVE THE RIGHT TO REMAIN SILENT!
AHHH!

KEEP BACK! OR I'LL...
EEEK! HEELLP!
ANNIE!
HELPLESS, huh?!
TASTE FIVE YEARS OF DANCE AEROBICS!!
Yiiii!!
TO ME, DOG BROTHERS! WE HAVE OUR PRIZES FOR KING ALBRECHT!

THEY VANISHED... LIKE THE VERY AIR!
Yeah. DON'T YOU HATE IT WHEN THAT HAPPENS?
SILVIA... THEY TOOK HER.
I WAS SO MEAN TO HER...
...AND SHE RAN TO SAVE ME.
AND THEY'VE SEIZED MJOLNIR, MY ENCHANTED HAMMER!
Oh, GOOD. OUR PRIORITIES ARE ALL IN ORDER!
COME ON, KID. WE'LL GET HER BACK ...ALONG WITH THE CONSTRUCTION TOOLS!
FATHER! GET UP! WE NEED ALL YOUR VAST WISDOM, ALL YOUR...
THERE WAS A LITTLE SMITHY...
...A HAPPY LITTLE SMITHY...

HOPELESS. WE HAVE TO FIGURE OUT WHERE THEY MIGHT HAVE GONE...
A JOLLY LITTLE SMITHY WAS HHEEEE...
ALBRECHT? WASN'T HE IN AN OPERA?
Aye. THE RING CYCLE.
IT WAS WRITTEN BY WAGNER FOR KING LUDWIG OF BAVARIA ...AND BASED TO A DEGREE ON OUR DOINGS IN ASGARD.
AND HIS JOLLY LITTLE ANVIL WENT "TUNK TUNK TUNK" AND HIS JOLLY LITTLE BELLOWS WENT "WHEEE..."
FATHER! BE SILENT!

WE WALK FOR THE BETTER PART OF THREE HOURS, UNFORTUNATELY NOT IN SILENCE. DO YOU KNOW HOW MANY VERSES THERE ARE TO "THE JOLLY LITTLE SMITHY"?
I DO.
I JUST DON'T GET IT, KIM. ALL SILVIA HAS WANTED IS FOR ME TO VANISH. AND I HATED HER. BUT...
YOU KNOW, ANNIE, PEOPLE AREN'T ALWAYS SIMPLE. IF...
HALLOO, MY GOOD FRIENDS!
A HOODED MAN!
I HAVE NEED OF AID. EVIL IS AFOOT AND I NEED HELP TO FIGHT IT. FOR I AM...
LOKI! EVIL INDEED! I'LL RIP YOUR HEART--
WAIT, THOR! HE SEEMS DIFFERENT!

PEACE, STRANGER! THOU MAY BE WROTH WITH ME, BUT I KNOW THEE NOT! MY BUSINESS IS ABOUT AN ILLNESS WHICH POSSESSES THE GODS!
KIM GAUNT IS RIGHT. THERE IS SOMETHING FINE, ALMOST NOBLE ABOUT THIS LOKI.
UNLESS SOMETHING BE DONE, ASGARD ITSELF IS DOOMED!
BUT, NO! SUCH NOBILITY IS NOT POSSIBLE IN HIM!
SPEAK QUICKLY, TRICKSTER! AND BE WARY! I WILL NOT BE GAMED WITH!
TRICKSTER I AM, BUT I CAN SEE THE VERY HEAVENS QUAKE WHEN THE GODS GO MAD FOR GOLD...
...NO!
AHHHH!
THK

THE ARROW CAME FROM UP... LOOK OUT, THOR!
DEATH TO THE ENEMIES OF ASGARD!
DEATH TO THE MUD-PEOPLE!
DEATH TO ALL WHO OPPOSE THE WILL OF WOTAN THE ALL-FATHER!
IT IS BALDER THE BRAVE! YET BALDER IS SUBTLY ALTERED... HIS FEATURES ARE TWISTED BY HATRED AND GREED! HOW IS SUCH A THING POSSIBLE?

YAAA! HHAA!
HAWWW!
THE HORSE REARS, STARTLED! THIS IS THE WAY LOKI AND I WOULD CATCH WILD PONIES ON THE PLAINS OF ASGARD WHEN I WAS A BOY!
BALDER IS STUNNED. IT WOULD BE CHIVALRY TO LET HIM REGAIN HIS FEET--TO GIVE HIM HIS WEAPON--TO FIGHT FAIR...
KRAK
...BUT WE ARE ALONE HERE, AND FOUR LIVES DEPEND ON MY BLADE, MY EXPERIENCE AS A WARRIOR. ONLY A FOOL IS CHIVALROUS IN SUCH A CASE.

Ahh...
SSKKRRRUP!
...YAAAA!
VICTOR PRAZNIKI, A MAN WHO RAN HIS OWN LABOR UNION FOR TWENTY YEARS, AND RAN HIS HOME AS IF HE WERE A GOD, IS LEARNING TODAY ABOUT THE LIMITS OF POWER.
Uh, LOKI...? Mr. LOKI, Sir...? HE'S JUST BEEN SITTING THERE FOR HOURS, STARING AT ME!
MEBBEE HE HAD A HEART ATTACK!
THOR, MY DAUGHTER ANNIE, ALL OF 'EM VANISHED WHEN THE OLD GUY GRABBED THE SWORD I BROUGHT TO LOKI FOR RANSOM.
I GOTTA GET HOLD OF THOR'S GIRL--THE ENCHANTRESS--SHE'LL KNOW WHAT TO DO...
THE COLD, STILL, ALMOST MECHANICAL EYES OF THE FROZEN GOD OF MISCHIEF BURNING INTO PRAZNIKI AS HE PUNCHES IN THE NUMBERS.
BE THERE, BE THERE...
HI. THIS IS THE ENCHANTRESS. WE'RE NOT HERE RIGHT NOW...

NEW YORK STATE PRISON...
HEY, THINKER! IF YOU C'N GET LONG DISTANCE REVENGE ON THOR FROM IN HERE, C'N YOU DO IT TO ANYBODY? 'CAUSE THERE'S A GUY...
THAT'S A GOOD IDEA. I GOTTA ASK THE MAD THINKER ABOUT THAT.
THINKER...?
HEY, GUARRRD! GET IN HERE! I THINK THE THINKER'S DEAD!

THE PROBLEM IS... HOW DOES ONE CAPTURE A PANICKING WINGED HORSE?
MY ANSWER:
BY SURPRISE!
AND THE ONLY THING TO BE WARY OF...
...IS THAT YOU ARE NOT THE ONE SURPRISED!

OR BITTEN!
OR THROWN!
OR ROLLED ON THE GROUND AND TRAMPLED!
YIKES! THOR, GET THAT THING OUT OF HERE!
GEEZ!
THEE SHALL NE'ER TAME MY FIERY STEED, MUD-THING!
SHALL I NOT--?
COME, HORSE! IF YOU WANT TO FLY... FLY!

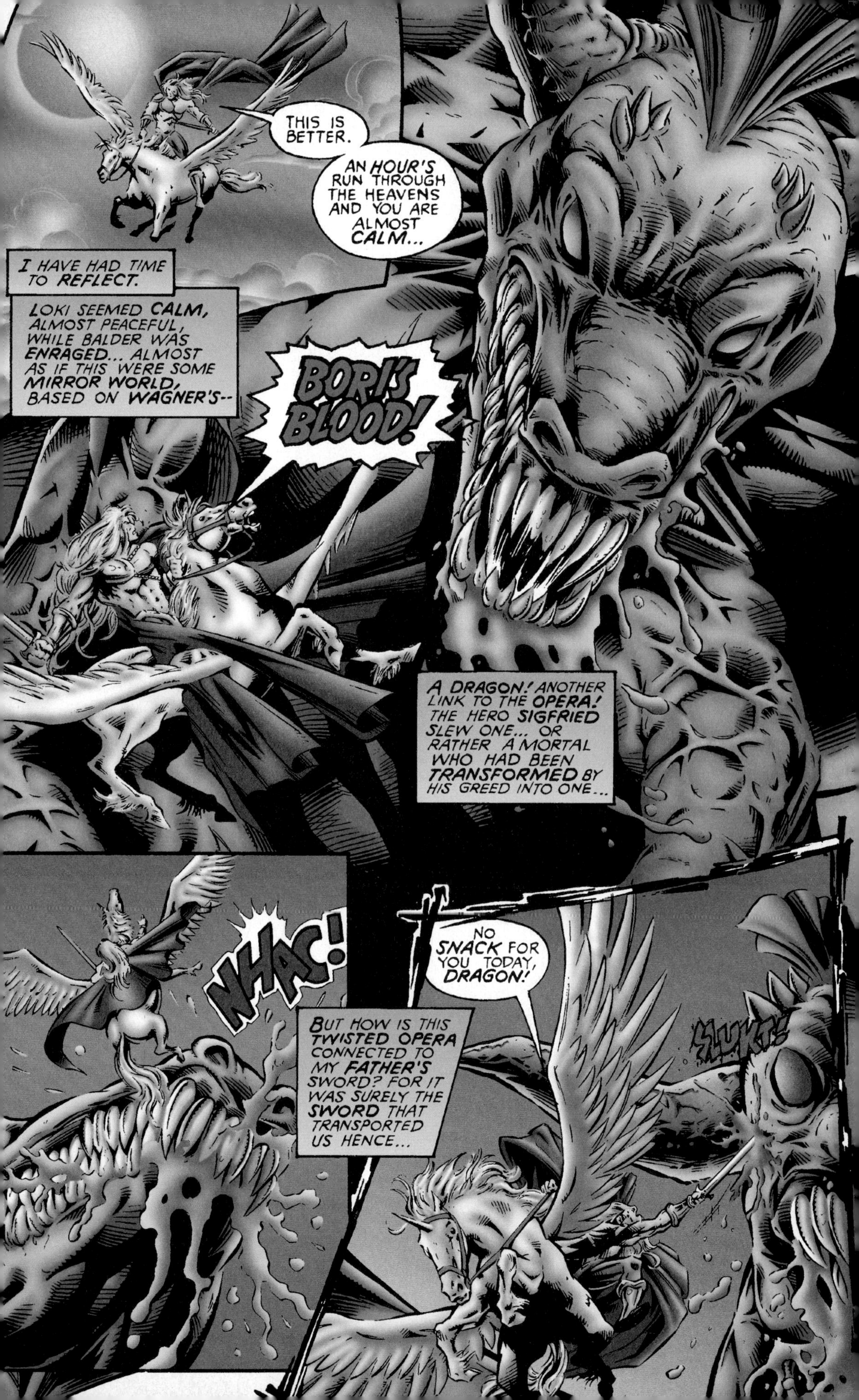
THIS IS BETTER.
AN HOUR'S RUN THROUGH THE HEAVENS AND YOU ARE ALMOST CALM...
I HAVE HAD TIME TO REFLECT.
LOKI SEEMED CALM, ALMOST PEACEFUL, WHILE BALDER WAS ENRAGED... ALMOST AS IF THIS WERE SOME MIRROR WORLD, BASED ON WAGNER'S--
BORI'S BLOOD!
A DRAGON! ANOTHER LINK TO THE OPERA! THE HERO SIGFRIED SLEW ONE... OR RATHER A MORTAL WHO HAD BEEN TRANSFORMED BY HIS GREED INTO ONE...
WHAC!
NO SNACK FOR YOU TODAY, DRAGON!
BUT HOW IS THIS TWISTED OPERA CONNECTED TO MY FATHER'S SWORD? FOR IT WAS SURELY THE SWORD THAT TRANSPORTED US HENCE...
SLUKT!

THE MONSTER FALLS, BUT NOT AS A DRAGON...
...AS A MAN!
KERASH!
MY GUESS IS I AM IN THE PRESENCE OF ALBRECHT, LATE KING OF THE DWARVES!
AND IF I REMEMBER THE TALE... THIS RING, FORGED OF RHINEMAIDEN'S GOLD, GAVE HIM THE SHAPESHIFTER'S POWER!
FLY HOME, BOY! WE'LL FIND THE ANSWERS THERE!

AN ELABORATE CASTLE, BUILT IN THE CLOUDS USING THE SWAN MOTIF BELOVED OF LUDWIG. MY GUESS IS... ASGARD!
BUT NOT THE ASGARD I KNOW. IT IS THE ASGARD IMAGINED BY WAGNER AND WOR-SHIPPED BY LUDWIG II OF BAVARIA.
VICTOR PRAZNIKI SAID THE SWORD HAD GONE FROM HAND TO HAND BEFORE HE GOT IT. SUPPOSE ONE OF THOSE HANDS WAS LUDWIG'S... HIS MADNESS WARPING WHAT-EVER MAGIC WAS ORIGINALLY IN THE SWORD?
CAN THE SWORD ITSELF HAVE THE POWER TO CREATE THIS WORLD, A MAD-MAN'S SKEWERED VISION OF REALITY? IMPOSSIBLE, AND YET HERE IT IS!
VOICES, THIS WAY...
NOW THAT WE HAVE ALL THE RHINE GOLD, THOR, MY SON... TRUE POWER IS OURS!
Aye, FATHER WOTAN! WE SHALL MAKE THE MUD-PEOPLE DANCE!
...THOR?
BRING IN THE PRISONERS!
HERE THEY ARE, WOTAN! THEY COULDN'T HOLD BALDER THE BRAVE!

YES! ALL OUR ENEMIES **FALL** BEFORE US!
AND I AM YOUR GOOD **RIGHT HAND,** FATHER! ONLY THOSE OF THE **TRUE BLOOD** SHALL RULE IN **ASGARD!**
*TRUE BLOOD? IS **THIS** HOW LOKI SAW MY FATHER AND ME? AS POSTURING MEGALO-MANIACS?*
ALL THE **DWARVES** ARE **SLAIN!** I GIVE THEM AS AN OFFERING TO YOUR **GREATNESS!**
NO!! THIS IS **EVIL!** I WILL HAVE NO PART IN SLAUGHTER! I WOULD RATHER BE **DEAD!**
PROPHETIC WORDS, **HALF-BREED** BROTHER!
*NO! WE WERE **NEVER** LIKE **THIS!***
BZZAAAKT!

NOW THERE IS MORE GOLD LEFT FOR THOSE OF US WITH PURE BLOOD!
AND YET, BALDER SEEMS TO HOLD HIMSELF EQUAL TO US, eh, FATHER?
INDEED!
NO MORE!
GOOD, SON! TEACH THE PRISONERS THE SAME LESSON!
NO!
I CANNOT LET THIS HAPPEN! AND YET WHAT WILL OCCUR WHEN A THOR OF ONE WORLD BATTLES THE THOR OF ANOTHER, THE NORNS ALONE KNOW!

BLOOD-MAD COWARD! YOU'LL HAVE TO GO THROUGH ME!
AS I WILL, MUD-ANIMAL!
WOOSH!
NOT TODAY!
IF NOBLE WOTAN WANTS AN OFFERING FROM ME, HE CAN TAKE MY SWORD--
--AND CHOKE ON IT!
URRRKKK!
IT IS AS THOUGH COLD STEEL SLIDES INTO MY OWN GUT! THIS IS NOT MY FATHER, AND YET THE SEEMING IS TRUE ENOUGH TO MAKE ME FEEL LIKE I AM HIS KILLER!
FLASH!

WHAT...? THIS IS MY ASGARD... BUT IN RUINS! WHAT MADNESS IS THIS?
YES, MY ASGARD. BUT MERE MONTHS AGO ASGARD WAS A BUSTLING METROPOLIS, FILLED WITH HAPPY PEOPLE.
WHAT HAS HAPPENED? THE WIDE STREETS ARE EMPTY, THE FOUNTAINS FILLED WITH OFFAL. THERE IS A MIASMA OF DECAY AND THE BUILDINGS HAVE TUMBLED IN UPON THEMSELVES, EVEN AS THE PAVING HAS BEEN HEAVED UP.
THERE ARE MARKS OF FIRE AND BLOOD ON THE WALLS. SMOKE CLOUDS THE AIR. WAR! WHO COULD HAVE BROUGHT SUCH UTTER DESOLATION TO MY CITY?
SOMEHOW, BY SLAYING THE FALSE ODIN, I WAS TRANSPORTED HERE... BY THE SWORD AGAIN PERHAPS. BUT THEN, WHERE ARE THE OTHERS?
I WILL KNOW WHAT IS HAPPENING TO ME AND REGAIN CONTROL OF MY DESTINY. I WILL SAFEGUARD THOSE WHO WERE PUT IN MY CARE. I WILL PLUMB THE DEPTHS OF THIS MYSTERY! THIS I SWEAR!

MARVEL COMICS

THOR

JULY '96 500

APPROVED BY THE COMICS CODE AUTHORITY

A MARVEL® 1ST! FANTASTIC 500TH ISSUE!

THOR

MIKE DEODATO JR.

DOUBLE-SIZED ISSUE!

THIS... CANNOT BE.
ASGARD IS IN RUIN! ITS HIGH SPIRES AND MAJESTIC WALLS ARE TOPPLED INTO RUBBLE.
AND THRUST UP THROUGH IT ALL, LIKE A LANCE, IS THE WORLD ASH, YGGDRASIL.
BUT THE ASH LOOKS POISONED, LEAFLESS AND DYING. EVERYWHERE I LOOK IS DECAY AND DISASTER. WHAT CALAMITY COULD THUS BRING DOWN THE HOME OF THE GODS?
WHAT TERRIBLE THING HAS HAPPENED HERE?
WM. MESSNER-LOEBS WRITER
MIKE DEODATO JR ARTIST
JONATHAN BABCOCK · LETTERING
MARIE JAVINS · COLOR ART
MALIBU · COMPUTER SEPARATIONS
BOBBIE CHASE · EDITOR
BOB HARRAS · EDITOR · IN · CHIEF...
...AND STAN LEE PRESENTS...
SUNLIGHT AND SHADOWS

MERE MOMENTS AGO I WAS IN A LAND OF MADNESS, WHERE THE STORIES THAT WAGNER WOVE ABOUT THE AESIR WERE BLENDED WITH THE FANTASIES OF HIS PATRON, MAD KING LUDWIG OF BAVARIA.

THE GODS THERE WERE TWISTED PARODIES OF US, WARPED BY BLOOD-LUST AND RAW POWER.

HERE WAS WHERE THAT VILE ODIN SAT, ORDERING THE DEATHS OF MY FRIENDS. I SPEARED THE TYRANT WITH THE ENCHANTED SWORD THAT BROUGHT US THERE.

NOW THERE IS NO TRACE OF THAT SWOR
NOR OF THE STRANGE ARMOR I WORE THER
NO TRACE. NOTHING BUT STONE...

WHAK
TROLLS.
LOOK, GAARK! I GOT HIM! THERE BE FREE VITTLES TONIGHT!
HE BE A BIG'UN, EKAK!
WE SHOULD TAKE THE TIME TO FLAY HIM. THERE BE TWO PAIR'A BOOTS IN THIS'UN!
...THOR?
SKRAKT

YOU WANT MY SKIN, WORM-SPITTLE? THEN TAKE IT-- AND BONE AND MUSCLE, TOO!
WOK WOK WOK WOK WOK WOK
TAKE IT AND CHOKE ON IT!
THIS BE OUR CITY NOW, MEAT! WE STOLE IT FAIR AND SQUARE!
WHAT IS TAKEN BY ARMS MUST BE HELD BY ARMS!
KEEP IT IF YOU CAN!

KRAK
THOOK
SWAK
HUF-HUF-HUFF!
TROLLS... HOW COULD SUCH A DEBASED PEOPLE INVADE ASGARD? AND NEVER COULD THEY CAUSE SO MUCH DAMAGE! AND WHERE ARE ALL THE DEFENDERS OF THIS PLACE?
THEY SAID THE GODS HAD VANISHED. WHAT SORCERY HAS TRANSPIRED SINCE MY BANISHMENT TO EARTH?

FOR A THOUSAND TIMES A THOUSAND YEARS, ASGARD HAS REMAINED UNCONQUERED-- SINCE MY FATHER CAUSED THESE WALLS TO BE RAISED.
BUT NOW IT IS ALL UNDONE AND...
PUT Y'R BACKS INTO IT, PRETTIES!
Ehh?
I WANT THIS ROAD CLOSED BY THE NOONTIDE, MOLLICODS!
I HEAR THE CRACK OF A WHIP, THE RATTLE OF CHAINS, THE GROAN OF HUMAN EFFORT, SOUNDS THAT HAVE BEEN FORBIDDEN HERE FOR CENTURIES...
...THE SOUNDS OF SLAVERY!
PUSH! PUSH-- CURSE Y'R SOFT HIDES!
AYE! IF THE INVADERS BREAK THROUGH HERE...

YOU'LL THINK WHAT WE DO TO YOU ONLY A LIGHT PLEASANTRY BY COMPARISON!
NO! THIS CANNOT BE!
FOR AS HORRIBLE AS I FIND CHATTEL SLAVERY BEING PRACTICED IN SACRED ASGARD, WHAT I SEE NOW IS A THOUSAND TIMES WORSE!
FOR I RECOGNIZE ONE OF THESE SLAVES...
...IT IS DR. STRANGE... SORCERER SUPREME OF ALL EARTH!

PERHAPS A DISTRACTION WILL AID ME IN SURPRISING THESE DIMWITTED CREATURES...
...OOPS! IT DIDN'T WORK!
THWAK
I AM NEARLY EXHAUSTED--
NO MATTER. I WILL BATTLE MY WAY THROUGH!
FOR ASGARD!
WHOK
--I HAVE BEEN FIGHTING FOR DAYS, AND...
HOLD HIM, BROTHER! I'LL FLAY HIM LIKE SUET!
NOT TODAY, YOU WON'T!
HELP ME, SOME OF YOU! WE CAN BE FREE!

BY THE IRON MOUNTAINS!
MY STRENGTH FAILS. WE ARE DOOMED.
BETTER TO DIE THAN LIVE LIKE THIS!
AIEE!
IT IS LIKE A DAM BREAKING...
GET THEM!
SMASH THE TROLLS!

NO MORE CHAINS! YOU ARE ALL FREE!
SHRAKT
TOGETHER WE CAN VANQUISH THE TROLLS AND RESTORE ASGARD! WHO IS WITH ME?!
Uh, WAIT...
...THE FIGHT IS THIS WAY...
OLD HOGNIR MIGHT AS WELL FIND THE TROLLS. I'LL BE DEAD SOON, ANYWAY.
WHERE ARE THE REST OF THE HUMAN AESIR?
MOST FLED TO THE HILLS WHEN THE GODS DISAPPEARED AND THE TROLLS CAME.

AND YOU, DOCTOR STRANGE. HOW CAME YOU HERE?
THAT, MY FRIEND, IS A LONG STORY...

"JUST YESTERDAY I WAS IN DEEP MEDITATION. I WAS ATTEMPTING TO DIVINE THE SOURCE OF A POWERFUL AND DISTURBING EVIL WHICH I'VE FELT WAS COMING FOR SOME LITTLE WHILE.
"IT IS AS THOUGH SOME DARK CLOUD HAS FALLEN ATHWART THE SUN, CASTING THE DESTINY OF ALL HUMAN-KIND INTO SHADOW.
"I SOUGHT TO LOCATE THIS EVIL, TO UNDERSTAND IT! BUT IT REMAINED ELUSIVE. AND THEN THE PHONE RANG.

"IT WAS THE ENCHANTRESS.

"SHE EXPLAINED THAT YOU HAD DISAPPEARED WHILE GUARDING THE WIFE AND DAUGHTER OF THE LABOR LEADER, VICTOR PRAZNIKI.
"AND THAT IT WAS CON-NECTED TO THE SWORD, RAVEN'S EYE

"GIVEN HER HISTORY, I FEARED A TRAP. STILL, HER LOVE FOR YOU WAS COMPELLING. AND SHE CAN BE MOST CONVINCING.
"A SIMPLE SPELL OF FINDING LED US TO THE SECRET ROOM WHERE YOU HAD FIRST BEEN. AND THERE BE-HIND THE DESK WAS THE FIGURE OF YOUR HALF-BROTHER, LOKI.
"IT WAS A ROBOT. A MECHAN-ICAL DECOY MEANT TO LURE YOU. IT HAD ABOUT IT STILL THE ESSENCE OF THE MAN WHO BUILT IT..."

"...THE MAD THINKER, WHO LAY IN HIS PRISON CELL, STILL WEARING HIS CYBER-CONTROLS, HIS MIND GONE.
"APPARENTLY, WHEN YOUR GROUP WAS TRANSPORTED BY THE SWORD, THE MYSTIC BLAST WAS SENT STRAIGHT TO THE THINKER'S BRAIN...
"...AND HIS MIND WAS SHATTERED.
"I SEARCHED THE WORLD AND BEYOND FOR YOUR ESSENCE...
"...AND WHEN I FOUND YOU IN ASGARD, THE ENCHAN-TRESS AND I FOLLOWED.
"BUT AS WE PASSED OVER THE RAINBOW BRIDGE, SOME GREATER MAGIC THAN MINE DISRUPTED OUR VOYAGE. WEAK AND HELPLESS, I FELL--
"--AND AWOKE THE NEXT DAY AMID TROLLS."
BUT THEN WHERE'S AMORA?
I DON'T KNOW, MY FRIEND...

"...BUT WHEREVER SHE LANDED, SHE'LL BE ALL RIGHT. SHE'S A SURVIVOR!"
YOU'RE GOING TO WAR WITH ASGARD...?
AYE, IT WILL BE A GREAT BATTLE! MANY OF THEM WILL DIE! MANY OF US WILL DIE! BLOOD WILL STAIN THE GROUND LIKE A SUNSET!
THEN I, SNAGG, SON OF BORT, SON OF HJAK, SON OF MOOT, LORD OF THE FROST GIANTS, WILL ALSO BE KING OF ASGARD!!
WHICH HAS BEEN OVERRUN BY THE TROLLS? SO YOU'RE GOING TO FIGHT A HUGE BATTLE OVER THE RUINS OF ASGARD, WHICH NEITHER OF YOU CAN ACTUALLY USE?

ANOTHER WAY? WE RUSH UPON THEM AND SLAY THEM! THEY RESIST AND KILL US! THERE ARE FEWER OF US BUT WE ARE LARGER AND HAVE MORE COURAGE!
I'VE NO LOYALTY TO AN ASGARD FILLED WITH TROLLS. PERHAPS I CAN HELP.
HELP? THOU ART TINY AND SOFT! THOU WILT HARDLY SURVIVE BEING A PARTY FAVOR AT THE VICTORY CELEBRATION!
NOW THERE'S AN IMAGE... BRR. WHAT IF I COULD SUGGEST AN EASIER WAY TO WIN?
SOON THERE WILL BE NAUGHT BUT A FIELD OF DEATH! A GRAND FEAST OF CARRION!
UH-HUH.
AS MUCH FUN AS THAT SOUNDS...
WHAT IF I COULD SUGGEST A LESS GRAND WAY...?

AND ELSEWHERE...
THIS IS TALLER THAN IT LOOKS!
SILVIA MAY STILL HAVE MARRIED DADDY FOR HIS MONEY, BUT I'M NOT GONNA LET HER ROT IN THIS 3-D VIDEO GAME!

OH-OH. WHERE ARE THEY GOING?
COME! THEY MAY BE BREAKING THROUGH THE MAIN GATE!

SILVIA!
SILVIA! ARE YOU IN HERE?

ANNIE...? HOW...?
I WAS WATCHING WHEN THEY MARCHED YOU IN HERE. TIME TO GO!

WHY HAVE YOU LOST YOUR MYSTIC POWERS, DOCTOR?
I WISH I KNEW! IT WAS ALMOST AS IF THEY HAD BEEN DRAINED OFF BY SOME GREATER FORCE.
WAIT! YOU HEAR THAT? A RUSHING NOISE, ALMOST LIKE A--
BWAM

A THOUSAND GENERATIONS OF HATRED BREAK FREE AS THE FROST GIANTS AT LAST BREACH THE WALLS OF ASGARD.
DEATH TO THE TROLLS!
WE SHALL BE KINGS OF THE WORLD!
THE GOLDEN CITY IS OURS!
I HOPE THIS STRANGE PLAN OF YOURS WORKS!
IT'S HARDLY COMPLEX. BESIDES, YOU WERE ALREADY PLANNING ON MOST OF YOUR MEN BEING SLAUGHTERED. HOW COULD THIS BE WORSE!
IT IS NEW!
HA! OVER HERE!
THOOM!
RIGHT HERE, FRIEND!
I HOPE DOC REMEMBERS THIS MOVE ...

AND THIS ENDS IT!
KILL THESE SMALL ONES!
NO... I CAN'T ALLOW...
--THIS!
SO POWERFUL IS EVEN A MINOR SPELL FROM THE SORCERER SUPREME THAT A DOZEN OF THE GIANTS ARE THROWN BACKWARDS AND THE WALL HEALED...
...BUT STILL MORE APPEAR!
COME ON! WE HAVE TO GET TO THE SHELTER!
HUH! WHAT IS THIS, THEN?

'TIS THE STING OF ULIK, LORD OF ASGARD.
TO ME, TROLLS! THROW BACK THE INTER-LOPERS!
THIS IS OUR OUR CITY NOW, GIANT!
THIS WAY, DOCTOR!
WHAT? THOR AND HIS FRIENDS FIGHTING FOR THE SAFETY OF ULIK?
AEE!!!!!
PRETTY UNBELIEVABLE, HUH?

THE ENCHANTRESS'S PLAN: WHILE ONE GROUP STORMS THE GATE, SEVERAL OTHERS SLIP OVER THE WALLS.
LOOK, TAROOK! A TINY GUARD! WHAT SHALL WE DO WITH HER?
OFFICER KIM GAUNT, NYPD, BOYS! AND YOU'RE BUSTED!
SHE'S INSANE! CRUSH HER!
UP AGAINST THE WALL AND SPREAD 'EM!
BLAM BLAM BLAM BLAM BLAM
AEEII! MY EYES!
EVIL MAGICKS!
YOU HAVE THE RIGHT TO REMAIN SILENT!

"ODIN, YOUR FATHER, IS THE KEY TO ALL THIS," DR. STRANGE EXPLAINS ONCE THIS BATTLE IS OVER. "HE CREATED THE SWORD. THE SWORD IS A TALISMAN."
"THEN MY FATHER CAN USE THE SWORD TO RESTORE ASGARD?" I ASK.
"I THINK NOT." STRANGE LOOKS WORRIED. "YOUR FATHER HAS BEEN ON EARTH A GOOD, LONG WHILE. HE MAY NOT EVEN REMEMBER THE SWORD."
I BEGIN TO BE AFRAID. "BUT... WHAT COULD HAVE BROUGHT HIM TO EARTH? AND WHAT HAPPENED TO THE OTHERS? WHAT POWER COULD REDUCE US ALL TO MORTALS?"
STRANGE SHRUGS.
"IF I HAVE TO GUESS... I'D POINT TOWARDS THE ASH TREE. ONLY IT HAS THE STRENGTH TO STRIP ME OF MY POWERS. YOU SAID IT WAS TRICKED INTO BELIEVING RAGNAROK HAD OCCURRED. WELL, BY ITS LIGHTS THERE SHOULD BE NO MORE GODS!"
"SO IT ELIMINATED THE GODS BY MAKING US ALL MORTAL? AND THEN WHAT? SENT US ALL TO EARTH?"
"I'D SAY THAT'S LIKELY. YOU, ODIN AND AMORA ALL ENDED UP THERE."
"THE SWORD IS PROBABLY STUCK IN A WALL OR A ROCK SOMEWHERE. THAT'S GENERALLY HOW MYSTIC BLADE PHYLACTERIES MANIFEST."
"ODIN MAY HAVE CREATED IT AS A CHARM WITHIN WHICH TO HIDE HIS ESSENCE UNTIL THE CRISIS PASSED."
THIS DID SOUND LIKE SOMETHING MY FATHER WOULD DO.
"BUT IT'S BEEN ON EARTH SINCE THE CRUSADES," I EXPLAIN.
"HOW BETTER TO SAFEGUARD IT THAN TO EMBED IT WITHIN HISTORY?"

THEN WE JUST HAVE TO PULL IT FREE?
FIRST WE HAVE TO FIND IT.
I... YOU AIDED ME, STORM GOD. THERE IS A SWORD. IT APPEARED IN THE SACRED ASH YESTERDAY.
THEN WE MUST GO TO THE SWORD!
YGGDRASIL NOW FORMS ONE SIDE OF THE RUIN THAT WAS THE PALACE.
WE MUST FIND MY FRIENDS BEFORE THE GIANTS DO.
BUT THERE IS NO NEED...
EVEN MY FATHER IS HERE!
AND THERE IS THE SWORD!
FATHER, YOU MUST TAKE UP THE SWORD AGAIN! YOU MUST...

HOPELESS...
SNOORRRPP
...THERE IS ONLY ONE CHANCE LEFT...
...BUT DO I HAVE MY FATHER'S STRENGTH...?
THE SWORD GOES TO ROT IN MY HAND.
BUT AM I ONCE AGAIN THE LORD OF THUNDER?
THE HAMMER...!
YES.

YES!
EVEN NOW I CAN HEAR THE FROST GIANTS BREAKING INTO THE PALACE.

PITY THE FROST GIANTS.
I SENT THEM THE LIGHTNING!
THE STORM...
...AND SCATTER THEM WITH THE HURRICANE...
...TO THE LAST MAN.

SHATTERED, THE REST OF THEIR ARMY TAKES TO ITS HEELS!
LEAVING A STRANGE, UNEASY CALM AFTER THE BATTLE.
I MUST RETURN TO EARTH. I MUST FIND MY PEOPLE. ULIK, KEEP THESE SHATTERED RUINS IF YOU WILL, BUT DO NOT HARM THE AESIR, OR...
IF THEY STAY AWAY WE WILL NO TOUCH THE THUNDERER
MY POWERS ARE RETURNING BY THE MINUTE, THOR. THAT'S GOOD, BUT...
...I HAVE A TERRIBLE PREMONITION OF DISASTER. HUMANITY IS IN TERRIBLE DANGER. I THINK WE'RE NEEDED.
AYE. WE MUST RETURN AT ONCE. OUR DESTINIES, WHATEVER THEY MAY BE, LIE ON EARTH!
THE BEGINNING!

ASGARD IS DESTROYED... AND WHERE ARE ALL THE GODS?

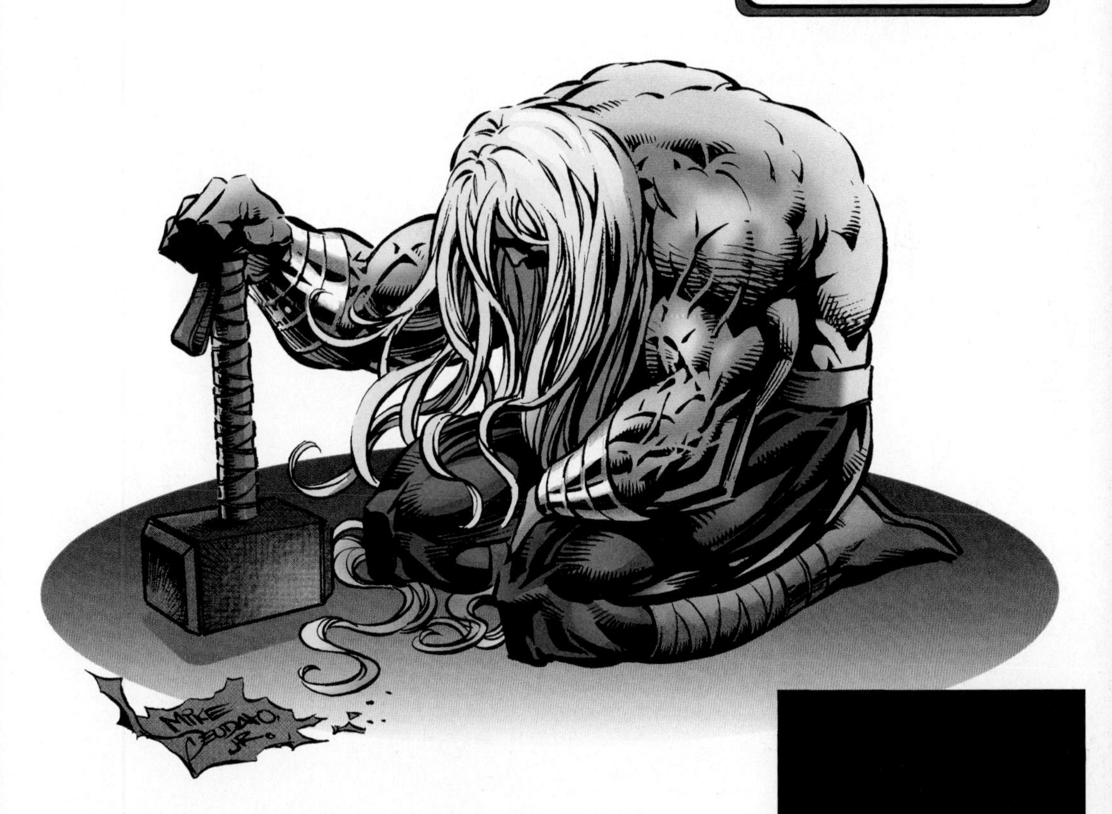

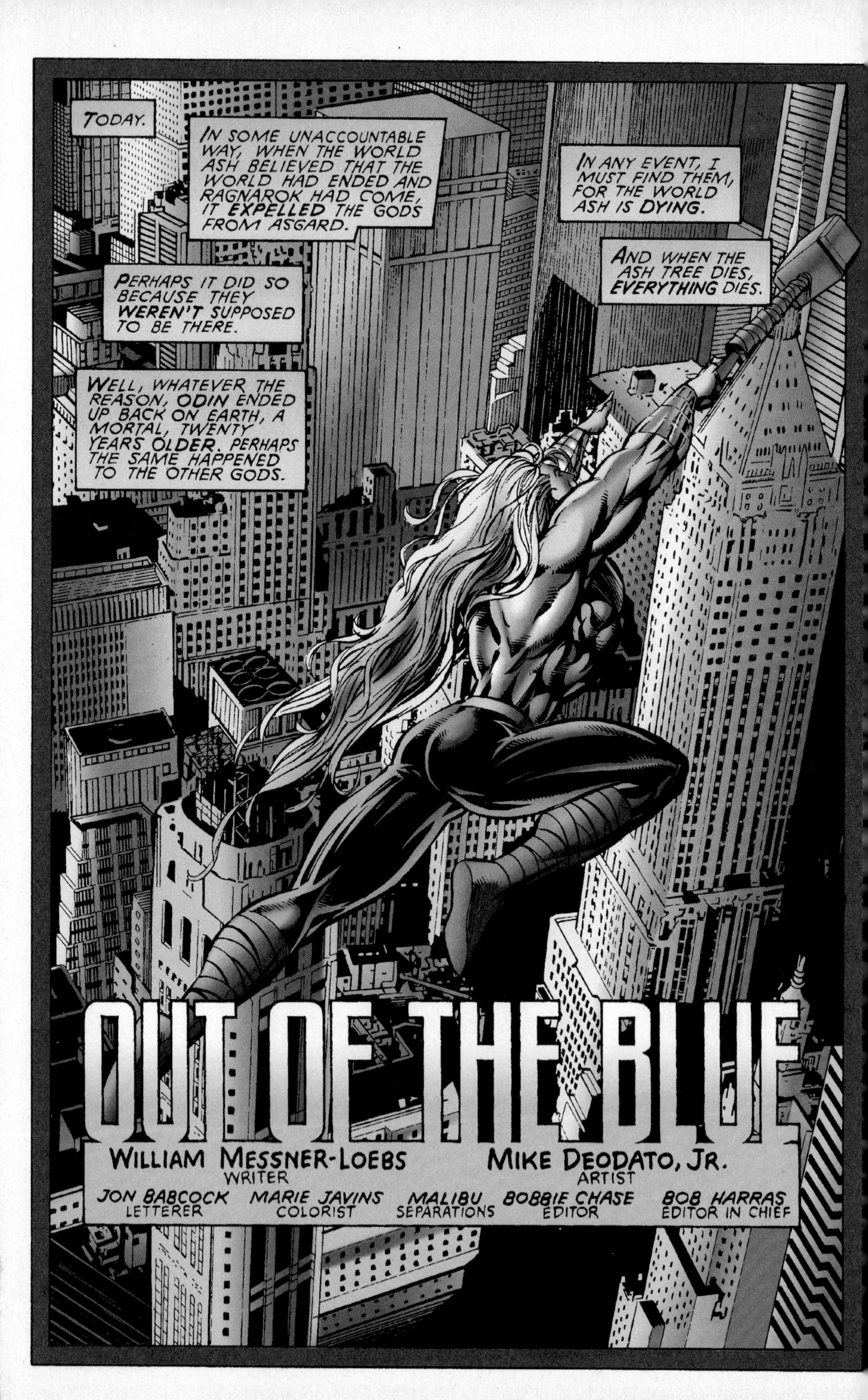
TODAY.
IN SOME UNACCOUNTABLE WAY, WHEN THE WORLD ASH BELIEVED THAT THE WORLD HAD ENDED AND RAGNAROK HAD COME, IT EXPELLED THE GODS FROM ASGARD.
PERHAPS IT DID SO BECAUSE THEY WEREN'T SUPPOSED TO BE THERE.
WELL, WHATEVER THE REASON, ODIN ENDED UP BACK ON EARTH, A MORTAL, TWENTY YEARS OLDER. PERHAPS THE SAME HAPPENED TO THE OTHER GODS.
IN ANY EVENT, I MUST FIND THEM, FOR THE WORLD ASH IS DYING.
AND WHEN THE ASH TREE DIES, EVERYTHING DIES.
OUT OF THE BLUE
WILLIAM MESSNER-LOEBS WRITER
MIKE DEODATO, JR. ARTIST
JON BABCOCK LETTERER
MARIE JAVINS COLORIST
MALIBU SEPARATIONS
BOBBIE CHASE EDITOR
BOB HARRAS EDITOR IN CHIEF

MY POWERS RETURNED WHEN I DREW ODIN'S BLADE FROM YGGDRASIL. Dr. STRANGE'S POWERS DID ALSO RETURN.
BUT ODIN'S DID NOT.
THUS STRANGE WAS ABLE TO RETURN TO EARTH. BUT THE ENCHANTRESS REMAINS AMONG THE MISSING. AND THE OTHER GODS...? ARE THEY TOO STILL POWERLESS?
A THOUSAND THOUSAND MORTALS LIVE AND WORK AND LAUGH AND LOVE HERE IN NEW YORK EVERY DAY. AND THIS IS JUST ONE CITY IN ONE CORNER OF ONE COUNTRY OF THE WORLD.
FINDING A HANDFUL OF MY FRIENDS AND FAMILY-- NOW MORTAL, AND SCATTERED THROUGHOUT THE PLANET-- SEEMS AN IMPOSSIBLE TASK.

STILL, I MUST TRY.
THE WORLD ASH HAS BEEN DAMAGED BY RECENT EVENTS, AND THUS BOTH ABSORBED AND MASKED STRANGE'S POWERS.
THUS, THE INFORMATION ON THINGS ASGARDIAN HE WAS ABLE TO GIVE ME WAS LIMITED.
BUT IN THIS CITY, THE PATHWAYS TO INFORMATION ARE MANY AND VARIED...
...AND THE FIRST PLACE TO START IS WITH THE POLICE.
HEY, BIG BOY' IS THAT A HAMMER IN YOUR POCKET, OR ARE YOU JUST GLAD TO SEE ME?
OFFICER KIM GAUNT SEEMS UTTERLY UNTOUCHED BY HER ADVENTURES IN ASGARD AND OTHER LEGENDARY REALMS.
I RAN THE NAMES YOU GAVE ME. NOTHING POPPED UP... EXCEPT THIS... ROGER "RED" NORVELL.
Hmmm. RED NORVELL. ONE OF THE MANY "THORS" CREATED BY MY FATHER TO PUNISH ME.
YOUNG Mr. NORVELL HAS QUITE A RECORD... MOSTLY BAR FIGHTS, D&D...
INDEED.
OVER THE LAST YEAR HE HAS FOUGHT WITH WITH EMPLOYERS, BOUNCERS, POLICE AND CAB DRIVERS...
HE'S HEADING NOWHERE FAST.
WANNA BITE?
NO, THANK YOU.
HE WORKS AS A FREE-LANCE CAMERAMAN FOR VARIOUS CABLE STATIONS...
...WHEN HE WORKS.

AND HE'S SEEING THE ESTRANGED WIFE OF JOHN DENNIS NASH, A.K.A. "JOHNNY THE GENT", PART OF THE LOCAL WILDLIFE.
YOU MEAN, HE IS A PART OF SOME CRIME FAMILY?
"A SMALL PART. EXTORTION AND LOAN-SHARKING MOSTLY, ADDED TO THE PART THAT HE'S CERTIFIABLY WHACKO."
"BY MY FATHER'S BLOOD! NORVELL MUST HAVE A DEATH WISH!"
"COULD BE. THERE'S A LOT OF THAT GOING AROUND."
I AM THE COUNT OF MONTE CRISTO! BRING ME THE HEADS OF THOSE WHO BETRAYED ME INTO PRISON...
BLAM
BLAM
BLAM
...OR DIE!!

WHAT IDIOCY...?
BLAMBLA
Woof.
THE LUNATICS ARE COMING OUT OF THE WOODWORK, LATELY!

LOOK AT 'EM SCATTER! THEY'RE ALL IN ON IT! ALL TRYING TO BETRAY ME!
STOP THIS!
AKOW
IT'S LIKE SOME EVIL MIND ORCE OR OMETHING S STIRRING 'EM UP!
I MUST DISCOVER WHERE THE OTHER ASGARDIANS MAY BE!
PERHAPS RED NORVELL HOLDS THE KEY!
GOOD LUCK!
GAUNT! THERE'S A CRAZY PERSON HOLDING HOSTAGES IN THE MIDTOWN SUBWAY!
CRIPES! IT NEVER ENDS.

RED NORVELL HATES ME.
NOT SURPRISING. WE WERE COMPETITORS FOR THE SAME GODHOOD. HE SAW ME AS AN UNGRATEFUL CHILD. I SAW HIM AS AN INTERLOPER.
IRONIC THAT WE SHOULD MEET AGAIN, NOT IN ASGARD, BUT IN THIS SMALL CORNER OF NEW JERSEY.
BORI'S BLOOD!
WHAT'S GONE ON HERE?
ON THE OTHER HAND, I WAS PROBABLY NOT HIS GREATEST CONCERN...
VELTA

APPARENTLY, SOMEONE-- OR SOMETHING-- FOUND HIM BEFORE I COULD.
IT LOOKS LIKE THEY-- OR IT-- FIRED A CANNON THROUGH HIS TRAILER.
YES, THIS IS THE RIGHT ADDRESS.
22511
BUT THERE IS NO SIGN OF LIFE.
WHATEVER FORCE DESTROYED RED NORVELL HAS GONE...
YOU?

WHAM
YESTERDAY.
THWA
WHAK
C'MON, NORVELL. PAY UP!
I... DON'T HAVE... THE MONEY...
TOO BAD.
LENNY BOFFO AIN'T LOANIN' CASH F'R HIS HEALTH.
KRAK
SLAM
YOU PAY UP THE 500 BUCKS AND WE DON'T HAVE TO COME BACK.
Yeah. WE GOT BETTER THINGS TO DO THAN SCREW WITH A LOSER LIKE YOU.

NO HARD FEELIN'S, RIGHT?
Yeah. BUSINESS IS BUSINESS.
I'M NOT A *LOSER*...
THWUMP
Yiii! HE'S NUTS!
I WAS A **GOD** ONCE!
AAARGH
THAK
Ahhhh, **SHADDUP!**
KRAK
Huh! TOUGH GUY!
THE *HEAT!* LET'S SPLIT!
SKREEEEEE

RED?
BREENA...?
ARE YOU OKAY? DID THEY HURT YOU?
Nah. I JUST... OWE 'EM... MONEY IS ALL...
THANK GOD! I THOUGHT THEY WERE FROM MY HUSBAND!
HUSBAND? YOU'RE MARRIED?
VRRRM VRRRM VRRRM
Uh-huh. KINDA.

Hi, Mr. NORVELL. MY NAME'S JOHN NASH. I HEAR YOU LIKE MY WIFE.
YOU'RE MARRIED TO JOHNNY THE GENT?
SEE, I C'N UNDERSTAND THIS. SHE'S A VERY PRETTY LADY.
BUT I GOT A REP IN THIS COMMUNITY. AND WHAT'S MINE IS MINE!
Ahhhhh!
PCHOW
PCHOW
PCHOW
PCHOW

COME ON, SABRINA. I FORGIVE YOU. I'M TAKING YOU BACK.
WHUMP
YOU'RE GIVING ME UP FOR THIS LOSER?
HE'S NOTHING!
HEY, JOHNNY. THE COPS.
WE'RE OUTTA HERE. I'LL FIGURE OUT WHAT TO DO ABOUT THESE DIRTBAGS LATER.
Mr. NORVELL?
I'M FROM THE STUDIO.
YOU DON'T LOOK LIKE A COP.

THIS IS A COURT ORDER. YOU'VE BEEN USING VIDEO EQUIPMENT YOU STOLE FOR MAKING PORNOGRAPHY. WE ARE HERE TO SEIZE THAT EQUIPMENT AND TO ENJOIN YOU FROM EVER SETTING FOOT INSIDE THE STUDIO AGAIN.
HEY! I JUST NEVER GOT AROUND TO RETURNING THAT CAMERA.
SOME FRIENDS OF MINE HIRED ME TO MAKE A PRIVATE ANNIVERSARY TAPE.
HOW WAS I TO KNOW THEY'D UP-LOAD IT TO THE INTERNET?
Geez. YOU DON'T HAVETA BREAK STUFF...
JUST A REMINDER FOR THE FUTURE, Mr. NORVELL. PRIVATE PROPERTY SHOULD BE RESPECTED.
Yeah. EVERYBODY'S PROPERTY BUT MINE.

SORRY I DIDN'T TELL YOU ABOUT JOHNNY, RED.
S'ALRIGHT, HON.

SEE, I LIKE YOU AN' EVERYTHING, BUT I RILLY NEED SOMEBODY WHO C'N PROTECT ME FROM JOHNNY.
cough
I CAN'T EVEN PROTECT MYSELF...

Uh-huh. I NOTICED. SO I WAS THINKIN'... WE HAD US SOME LAUGHS, BUT...
Oh, MAN. YOU'RE BREAKING UP WITH ME? WHAT ELSE C'N HAPPEN TODAY?

SKRAAKA
BOOM
AND, HALF A UNIVERSE AWAY, ON ASGARD, THOR PULLS AN ENCHANTED SWORD FROM THE WORLD ASH AND REGAINS HIS POWERS.
RED, HONEY, I THINK YOU JUST GOT HIT BY LIGHTNING!

RED... Y'R CUTS AND BRUISES ARE ALL GONE!
HEY, I FEEL GREAT!
IT HAPPENED! I'M THOR AGAIN!
I WASN'T NUTS! IT ALL REALLY HAPPENED!
SEE, I WAS THIS GOD OF THUNDER ON ASGARD! AND I HAD THIS HAMMER. ALL I HAD T'DO WAS THINK AND IT'D JUMP RIGHT TO ME!
Geez, RED, HONEY! Y'S SO... BIG!
"THEN, A YEAR AGO I WOKE UP IN THE OCEAN, ABOUT A MILE OFF SHORE. MY POWERS... EVERYTHING... GON
"YOU KNOW WHAT A COMEDOWN THAT IS? TO BE A GOD AND THEN BE A NOBODY?
"ANYHOW, I SWAM TO SHORE, BUT I NEVER DID FIND THE HAMMER. IT MUST'VE SUNK WITHOUT A TRACE.

"I CALLED IT AND CALLED IT, AND NOTHING HAPPENED. I WASN'T THOR. I WASN'T ANYTHING!
WHO CARES ABOUT A HAMMER? YOU'RE SOMETHING NOW!
I GUESS I AM.
WHOOOOSSSSSHHH
"NOW IT'S TOO FAR AWAY."
DID YOU HEAR...? RUN, BREENIE! WE GOTTA GET OUT'A THE--

KRROOOOOOOOOOOOOM!!
WHOOOOOF!
THE HAMMER CAME BACK...
...COOL!

TODAY.
SO... WHADDAYA THINK?
RED NORVELL?

I KNOW THEY AREN'T REALLY AUTHENTIC, BUT WHEN I GET BACK TO ASGARD--!
THERE IS NO ASGARD.
OR RATHER IT IS A RUIN CURRENTLY BEING FOUGHT OVER BY GIANTS AND TROLLS.
SOUNDS LIKE I'VE BEEN OUT OF THE LOOP FOR A WHILE!
HOLD STILL, HONEY.
SO WHAT'S ODIN GOT TO SAY ABOUT ALL THIS?
Yiiii!
ODIN?
YOU SAID HIS NAME.
I LEFT HIM WITH Dr. STRANGE, BUT OBVIOUSLY WE ARE ALL LINKED TOGETHER SOMEHOW.
HE DOESN'T SEEM MUCH LIKE A GOD. PEE-YEEW!
MORE IMPORTANTLY, ALL THE GODS ARE HERE ON EARTH. SOMEHOW THE WORLD ASH CAST THEM OUT JUST AS IT DID YOU.

WE MUST SEARCH THIS COUNTRY AND FIND THEM, ELSE THE BALANCE OF ASGARD WILL NEVER BE *RESTORED!*
Uh, RIGHT.
"WE"?

TOMORROW.
THIS IS HOPELESS! OUR ARMY IS SCATTERED, PYLLAR!
KEEP SEARCHING, MROHT! WE NEED WEAPONS!
AYE. WHAT ARE FROST GIANTS WITHOUT WEAPONS?!
THOUGH WE WERE DEFEATED BY THE FURY OF THE THUNDER GOD, IF WE BUT HAD SWORDS...
LOOK WHAT I FOUND, PYLLAR! CAN I KEEP HER?
To Be Continued...

Thor #499, page 3
art by Mike Deodato Jr.

Thor #500, page 10
art by Mike Deodato Jr.

Thor #502 tied in to the 1996 "Onslaught" crossover, featuring the psionic villain overrunning Manhattan with scores of mutant-hunting Sentinels. Onslaught was defeated in *Onslaught: Marvel Universe* — but Thor, the Avengers and the Fantastic Four were sucked into a pocket dimension for a lengthy period of time and presumed dead by the Marvel Universe. *Thor #502* was the title's final issue until the 1998 "Heroes Reborn" reboot.

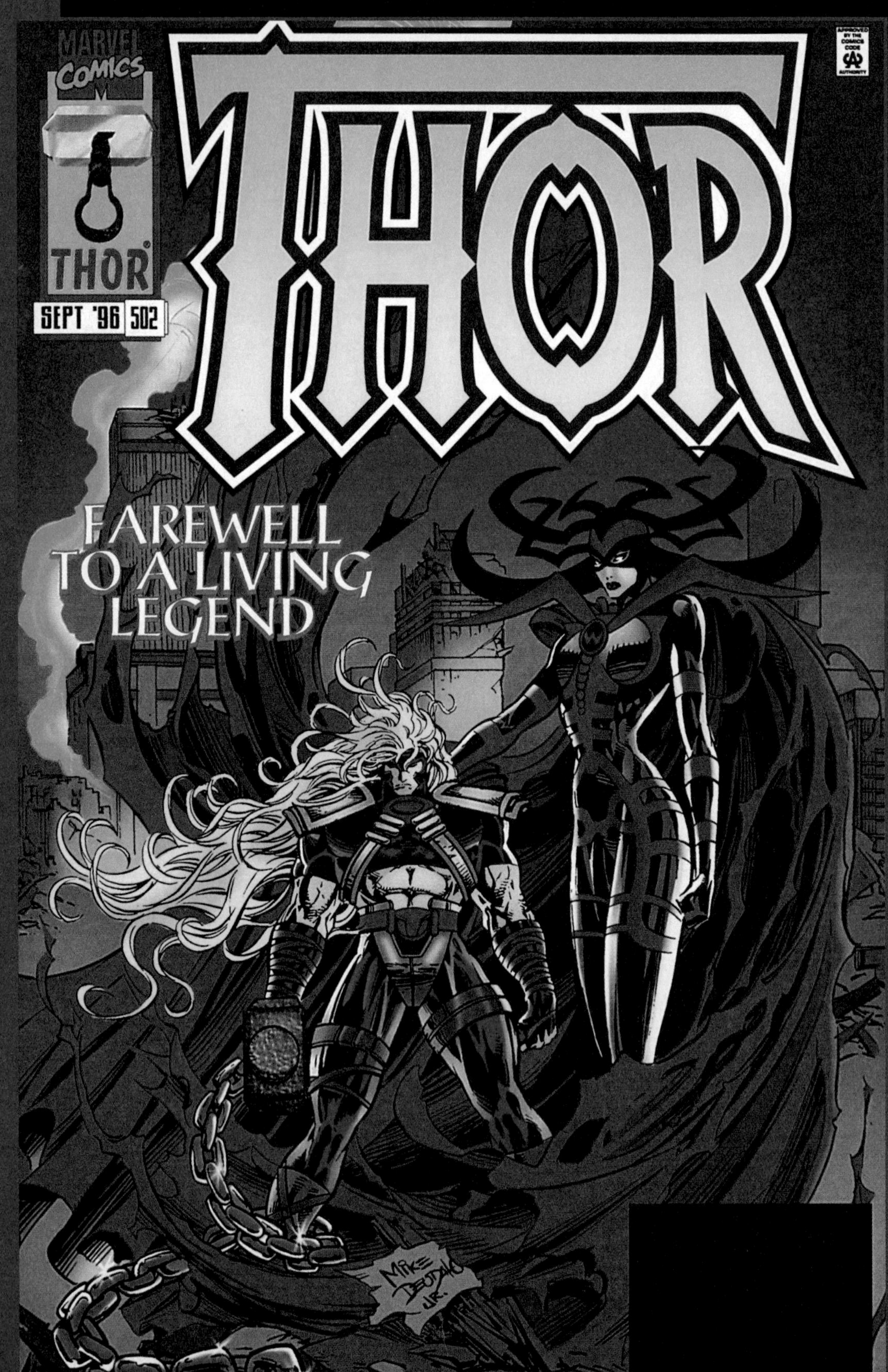

IT WAS THREE DAYS AGO THAT WE RAN FROM NEW YORK, GIVING ONSLAUGHT HIS FIRST VICTORY, AND CONTROL OF THE FATE OF EIGHT MILLION SOULS.*
SINCE THEN WE HAVE BEEN LIVING LIKE RATS ON THE JERSEY SHORE, ALONG WITH MOST OF THE POPULATION OF THREE STATES. ALL HAVE BEEN STRIPPED OF THEIR POWER BY THE ELECTROMAGNETIC PULSE CREATED BY OUR FOE.
RED NORVELL, A HUMAN GIFTED WITH POWERS THE EQUAL TO MINE, THE POWERS OF THOR, HAS STAYED WITH ME, AS WE PLAN OUR NEXT MOVE...
THOR... I HEARD YOU LAST NIGHT...CHANTING. SOUNDED LIKE MAGIC.
OF A SORT. I WAS TRYING TO INVOKE BERSERKER RAGE. THAT'S THE MINDLESS BATTLE PASSION THAT INCREASES THE WARRIOR'S STRENGTH TENFOLD.
Uh-huh. ANY LUCK?
MY BLOOD REMAINS AS COOL AS ICE. ALTHOUGH THE RAGE MAY BE MY ONLY HOPE IN DEFEATING ONSLAUGHT, I CANNOT BRING IT ON. PERHAPS AFTER YEARS OF TRYING I HAVE FINALLY BECOME HUMAN...
...TOO HUMAN TO FIGHT AS A GOD MUST FIGHT!
BILL MESSNER-LOEBS WRITER
MIKE DEODATO JR. PENCIL ART
DEODATO STUDIOS INKS
J. BABCOCK: LETTERS
MARIE JAVINS: COLORS
MALIBU: COLOR ENHANCEMENTS
BOBBIE CHASE: EDITOR
BOB HARRAS: EDITOR IN CHIEF
STAN LEE PRESENTS...
PUTTING ON THE BEAR SHIRT
*FOR ONSLAUGHT EVENTS LEADING UP TO THIS, SEE UNCANNY X-MEN #336!

BUT DIDN'T YOU START OUT AS A HUMAN, LIKE I DID? I THOUGHT I HEARD--
INDEED, I WAS HUMAN FOR A TIME... BUT NOT QUITE LIKE YOU, RED.
I LIVED FOR YEARS ON EARTH, A MAN LIKE OTHER MEN.
MY NAME WAS DONALD BLAKE.
I WAS A DOCTOR, A HEALER, ALTHOUGH I COULD NOT HEAL MYSELF.
I BELIEVED MY LAMENESS MADE ME UNLOVABLE...
...ESPECIALLY TO JANE FOSTER, WHO WORKED BESIDE ME IN THE CLINIC.
I LOST MYSELF IN WORK...
...AND IN DREAMS OF THE PAST. I DIDN'T KNOW WHY, BUT I WAS OBSESSED WITH MY SCANDANAVIAN HERITAGE.
I SPENT EVERY SPARE MOMENT LOST IN THE STUDY OF NORSE MYTH AND LEGEND.

AT LAST I WAS ABLE TO AFFORD A TRIP TO THE BLEAK HILLS AND TWISTED FJORDS OF NORWAY.
MUCH TO MY SURPRISE, JANE CAME WITH ME.
LITTLE DID I REALIZE SHE LOVED ME.
I WAS TOO LOST IN MY OWN DRIVEN MISERY TO SEE HER LOVE FOR ME.
ONE DAY I BECAME CONFUSED WHILE HIKING AND STUMBLED UPON AN ANCIENT CAVE.
WITHIN THE CAVE WAS A CANE, WITH RUNES CARVED INTO IT.
I STRUCK IT ON THE GROUND...
...AND ALL THE POWER OF THE UNIVERSE FLOWED THROUGH ME.

I WAS THOR, GOD OF THE STORM!
I CONTROLLED THE LIGHTNING...
...AND THE GREAT WINDS!
I HAD BECOME THE PERSONIFICATION OF STRENGTH AND BRAVERY... THE PROTECTOR OF THE EARTH!

AS IT TURNED OUT ALL MY MEMORIES OF "DONALD BLAKE" WERE GIVEN TO ME BY THE ALL-FATHER, ODIN, IN AN ATTEMPT TO TEACH ME HUMILITY.
I FOUND THIS OUT MUCH LATER.
ODIN HAD GIVEN ME A FALSE LIFE, BUT HAD NOT COUNTED ON THE ATTACHMENTS I WOULD FORM BECAUSE OF IT.
I PETITIONED ODIN TO MAKE JANE AN IMMORTAL, BUT HE FOUND HER WANTING AND SENT HER AWAY...
...WHILE I DID NOTHING.
NOW ODIN IS SO CHANGED THAT I...
FATHER...?
CRUNCH crunch GULP

FATHER, WHAT HAS HAPPENED TO YOU? HOW DID YOU GET THIS WAY?
EVERYTHIN' WAS TERRIBLE... THORS ALL WERE DYING. EVERY DAY MORE OF MY PEOPLE WOULD VANISH... NOTHING I COULD DO... RAGNAROK WAS COMING...
"...I FILLED MY SWORD RAVENSEYE WITH MEMORIES OF OUR LIFE IN ASGARD--
--AND HURLED IT OVER THE RAINBOW BRIDGE, INTO THE SWIRLING CHAOS BELOW.
"I WAS ALONE IN A DESERTED AND CRUMBLING ASGARD. WEARINESS OVERTOOK ME AND I SLEPT WHERE I FELL.
"ONLY TO AWAKE IN A STINKING ALLEY AMONG THE HUMANS. MY ARMOR, JEWELS, WEAPONS AND BOOTS HAD BEEN STRIPPED FROM ME WHILE I SLEPT!"

"I WAS COMPLETELY ALONE.
"NO ONE WORSHIPPED ME.
"AFTER MILLENNIA OF WORSHIP, NO ONE CARED IF I LIVED OR DIED.
I AM ODIN! I GAVE YOU LIFE!
WHAT ARE YOU HIGH ON, OLD MAN?
"I WAS MOCKED...
"...AND INSULTED.
WE DON'T WANT YOUR KIND HERE, HIPPIE!
"I WAS SUITED FOR ONLY THE LOWLIEST PHYSICAL LABOR...
"...AND DISCOVERED THAT THE MEAD IN THIS WORLD WAS ESPECIALLY POTENT.
GOD IS DEAD --NIETZCHE
"IT COULD BRING A MEASURE OF PEACE AND, AT LAST, OBLIVION."

HE WAS THROWN DECADES INTO THE PAST? WHY DIDN'T HE APPROACH ME WHEN I FIRST CAME TO EARTH?
WHY DIDN'T I? WHO WANTS TO BE SEEN AS A FAILURE?

I THINK I ATE A BUG.

CAN'T YOU GET BACK TO ASGARD NOW THAT YOU'RE UP TO SPEED AGAIN?
NO, NOT WITH THE RAINBOW BRIDGE DESTROYED. IT WOULD TAKE WEEKS.

AND BEYOND THE FIELDS WE KNOW...
COMPANY, PYLLAR! THAT'S WHAT SHE IS!
Y'R RIGHT, MROHT! FIGHTIN' MEN SUCH AS WE NEED A LITTLE WOMAN T'BRING OUR SPOILS TO!

SHE'S PLENTY LITTLE!
I DON'T UNDERSTAND.

THERE MUST BE MORE TO LIFE THAN GRUEL AND ENDLESS DRUDGERY.
YET I CAN'T REMEMBER EVEN MY OWN NAME!

AND YET I FEAR AMORA IS TRAPPED IN THAT BATTLE-GROUND.
PERHAPS SHE IS SAFER...
Uh, PAL? LOOKS LIKE WE HAVE COMPANY!

BE SURE THESE ARE SCRUBBED WELL, GIRL! WE CAN'T TRADE 'EM 'LESS THEY'RE CLEAN.

Yep. IT'S GOOD TO HAVE A WOMAN T'SUPPORT!
I JUST HOPE SHE KNOWS HOW GOOD SHE'S GOT IT!

Ahh, THAT WAS A GOOD LOOTING EXPEDITION, eh, BROTHERS?
Aye. I LIKE FIGHTING TROLLS!
THEY POP SO... DO YE HEAR THAT?
MANY YEARS AGO. A CREW OF FROST GIANTS, LOADED DOWN WITH BOOTY, MEANDER THROUGH THE ENCHANTED WOODS...
HELP ME... Oh, Please... HELP ME!
THNAT WILL "SAVE" YOU, PRETTY LADY! snicker
NOW, GOLDILOCKS! HURRY UP! NOW!
THWOK

TIME FOR LEAVE-TAKING!
I REMEMBER THE PLAN, LOKI!
HAVE TO BE FASTER THAN THAT TO CATCH ME!
ARE YOU BACK AT THE TRIP-ROCK, THOR?
AVALANCHE! HELP!
RUN! AIIIIEEEE!
HERE'S A SPELL FOR YOUR TROUBLE!
C'MON!
DON'T WAIT FOR ME!
Oh-oh! LOOKS LIKE THEY DON'T HAVE PONIES TO RIDE! WE WIN!
GET THEM! IT WAS A TRICK!
A-HA HA HAH! HAHA-A-HA HA HA HAHAHA HA!
A-HAHA HAHA!
HE'S GOT A STRONG GRASP OF THE OBVIOUS, DOESN'T HE?
EVEN TODAY, I CAN REMEMBER THE SMELL OF THE AIR, AND THE SOUND OF LOKI'S WILD LAUGHTER.

WE EXPECTED TO BE HEROES, BUT...
LOOK AT OUR BOOTY! WE THOUGHT YOU'D BE PLEASED...!
B-BUT, FATHER...
RASCALS! DOLTS!
NO SOONER HAD I NEGOTIATED PEACE WITH THE FROST GIANTS, THAN MY OWN SONS EMBARRASS ME THIS WAY!
HOW DARE YOU?
LOKI! THOU ART ALWAYS IN TROUBLE! IS THIS MY THANKS FOR TAKING THEE IN?
AND THOR! I KNEW THOU HADN'T MANY BRAINS!
STILL, I EXPECTED BETTER OF THEE.
WE WERE CONFINED TO THE PALACE FOR A MONTH AND FORCED TO SCRUB DOWN THE STABLES WITH CURRY BRUSHES. STILL...
...FROM ALL MY BOYHOOD, THAT DAY IS MY HAPPIEST MEMORY.

THOR? DO YOU KNOW *WHY* WE'RE COVERED IN *FROGS*?
LOKI WAS *ALWAYS* GETTING ME INTO *TROUBLE*. I WISH I HAD JUST ONCE TOLD HIM HOW MUCH I *ENJOYED* IT.
THE NOTES OF ONSLAUGHT'S MADNESS HAVE REVERBERATED EVEN THROUGH THE PONDS AND FENS OF *THEIR* WORLD...
...I SUSPECT THEY'RE HERE TO SAY *GOOD-BYE*.
RIGHT. LIKE YOU CAN *TALK* TO FROGS!
Cheepie-Cheepie, l'il fellow...
CHEERRUP
CHEERRUP
CHEERRUP
CHEER
Yiiii!
CHEERRUP
CHEERRUP
CHEERRUP
CHEERRUP
CHEERRUP

SORRY. DIDN'T MEAN TO UPSET EVERY-ONE.
JANE.
CAP TOLD ME YOU WERE CAMPING HERE. HOW'S IT GOING, BOYS?
BADLY.

ONSLAUGHT OWNS NEW YORK, AT LEAST FOR THE MOMENT. WE DON'T KNOW IF WE CAN WIN THIS ONE.
WHY ARE YOU HERE?
THERE HAVE BEEN SO MANY CASUALTIES. I FIGURED THEY COULD USE AN EXPERIENCED NURSE.
I'M GLAD I WAS ABLE TO FIND YOU. I SAID SOME THINGS BEFORE, DONALD...
SORRY. I'VE NEVER QUITE ACCEPTED THAT DON BLAKE WASN'T REAL.
HE WAS... WITH YOU.
I DIDN'T WANT... THINGS TO END THE WAY THEY DID... WHAT WE HAD... WHAT WE WERE...

LOOK WHAT I FOUND WANDERING AROUND IN THE STREET.
POWER... CUT OUT... CAR CRASHED...
DADDY...?
SO COLD... =cof=
...HURT...
HE'S IN SHOCK. HE NEEDS A HOSPITAL.
YOU KNOW WHERE ONE IS AROUND HERE? I SURE DON'T.
IS HE GONNA DIE?
NOT IF WE CAN HELP IT. I PACKED SOME STUFF...
WERE YOU PLANNING ON OPEN-ING A CLINIC?
I FIGURED SUPPLIES WOULD BE LOW. READY FOR SOME MEAT-BALL SURGERY, DOCTOR...?
LOOKS LIKE WE HAVEN'T MUCH CHOICE.
WE NEVER SEEM TO.
RED... TAKE THE YOUNG LADY FOR A WALK, WILL YOU?

IT'S BEEN A LONG TIME SINCE I DID THIS... HELD A MAN'S LIFE IN MY HANDS.
IT FEELS GOOD.
BUT THEN WE ALWAYS DID. IT WAS OUTSIDE THE OFFICE WE NEVER SEEMED TO GET STRAIGHT.
RIGHT.
JANE AND I WORK TOGETHER AS ONE.
THE BLEEDING'S STOPPED.
WHO CAN YOU PRAY TO... WHEN YOU'RE THE RELIGION?
MISTER? ARE YOU THOR TOO?
Nah. HE'S THE GOODS. I'M THE BEST FRIEND.
THAT IS ALL WE CAN DO HERE. HE NEEDS AN E.R.

WE DID IT!
'COURSE WE DID. WE'RE A GREAT TEAM.
Well... I SHOULD PROBABLY GO WITH THEM TO THE HOSPITAL.
YES. YOU SHOULD PROBABLY GO...
FORTY-FIVE MINUTES LATER, WE FIND A WORKING PHONE AND CALL AN AMBULANCE.
HALF AN HOUR AFTER THAT ONE ACTUALLY ARRIVES.
JANE LEAVES WITH IT.
IT'S CALLED "PUTTING ON THE BEAR SHIRT".
WHAT?
THE BEAR SHIRT. BEAR-SERKER, YOU SEE? A STATE OF TOTAL RAGE AND STRENGTH.
AND NO MIND.
IF I HAD BECOME BERSER-KER, I WOULDN'T HAVE BEEN ABLE TO HELP THAT MAN. HE WOULD'VE DIED. SO IT WAS ALL FOR THE BEST AFTER ALL.
DID I EVER MENTION THAT I WAS PROUD TO KNOW YOU?

THE RIVER'S BOILING. THERE'S SOMETHING YOU DON'T SEE EVERYDAY.
Well, IT IS THE EAST RIVER...
ALL RIGHT. IT IS SOMETHING YOU SEE EVERY-DAY. STILL...
HEL.

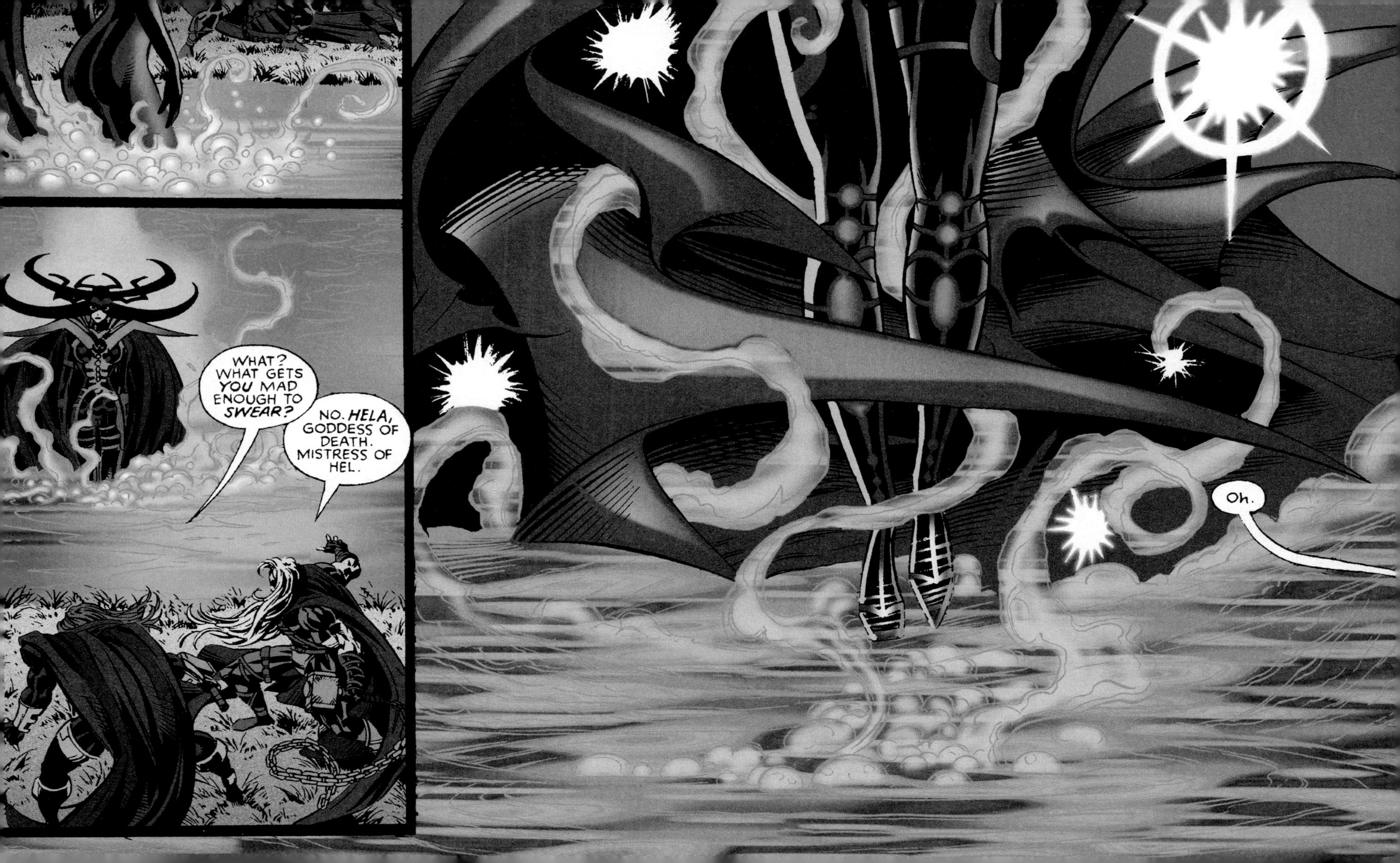
WHAT? WHAT GETS *YOU* MAD ENOUGH TO *SWEAR?*
NO. *HELA,* GODDESS OF DEATH. MISTRESS OF HEL.
Oh.

WHAT'S HAPPENING?
THERE'S A VOICE... FEELINGS IN MY MIND. I THINK IT'S AN OFFER.
SHE'S SAYING I WILL DIE TOMORROW, TO GO INTO OBLIVION AND NULLITY. BUT IF I GO WITH HER TONIGHT, I WILL BE HER MATE... FOREVER.
PRINCE OF THE DEAD.
WHAT'S HAPPENING NOW?
I'M THINKING IT OVER.

WELL, WE SHOULD GET SOME SLEEP. BIG DAY TOMORROW.

GOOD SOUVLAKI.
LUCKY THING DEMETRIS' HAD DRY ICE FOR REFRIGERATION.

THOR... WITH ALL YOU KNOW... WITH EVERY-THING THAT COULD HAPPEN TOMORROW... IF YOU HAD IT TO DO OVER AGAIN...?

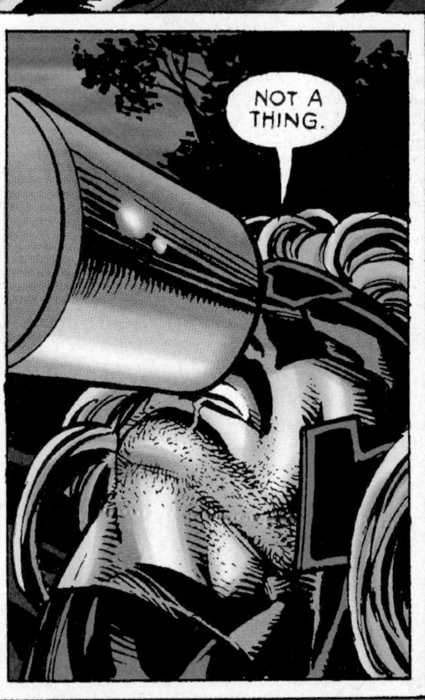
NOT A THING.

GOOD.
END.

THOR QUIZ

Hey, hammerbrain! How well do you know the God of Thunder and his mighty mythos? Test the Thor-oughness of your knowledge of all things Asgardian with the ten brain-rippers below!

1

Thor's gone by more aliases than a CIA operative. Which is not one of his phony names?

A. Donald Blake
B. Siegfried
C. Snorri Sturluson
D. Sigurd Jarlson

2

Thor's father is Odin. Thor's mother is...

A. Frigga B. Jord C. Sigyn
D. Apparently some kind of bird. Was he born wearing that winged helmet or what?

3

The name Asgard means...

A. Realm of the Aesir
B. Cool, dry armpits—no matter what the weather!
C. Land of the Warriors
D. Fields of Heaven

4

Thor's evil brother Loki has done a lot of rotten things, but he's never stooped to...

A. Lopping off Sif's hair
B. Masterminding "acts of vengeance"
C. Usurping the throne of Asgard
D. Trashing the Rainbow Bridge

5 With which of the following babes has Thor never locked lips?

 A. Sif

 B. Jane Foster

 C. Karnilla

 D. The Enchantress

6 In a fit of inspiration, Odin built a massive metallic construct to serve as invincible armor to battle the Celestials. We know it as....

 A. The Punisher

 B. The Destroyer

C. Something that dentists call "headgear"

 D. Thermal Man

7 One of these guys has never lifted Thor's hammer. The "pansy" is...

A. Hercules

 B. Odinson

 C. Eric Master-

 D. Captain America

8 Who is not one of the Warriors Three of Asgard (but would be available to make a fourth for bridge)?

 A. Volstagg

 B. Hogun

 C. Balder

 D. Fandral

9 The Thor Corps was made up of various counterparts of Thor throughout time and space. Which of the following was not a member?

 A. Dargo

 B. Beta Ray Bill

 C. Thunderstrike

 D. Red Norvell

10 Thor's swapped blows with enemies ranging from egg-shaped spacemen to dragons the size of the Chrysler Building. But when he's in the mood for a little down-home butt-kicking, he heads straight for the Asgardian-born...

 A. Absorbing Man

 B. Grey Gargoyle

 C. High Evolutionary

 D. Executioner

Answers on Page 47

the GARB of

When he busted his first move in a Marvel comic over 30 years ago, the mighty Thor was wearing the same clothes he had worn for over a thousand years.

FIRST SEEN IN JOURNEY INTO MYSTERY #83, THIS UNIFORM WOULD DEFINE THE THUNDER GOD'S LOOK FOR YEARS TO COME.

Suffering from a curse that made his bones brittle (as well as from extensive dry-cleaning bills), Thor forged himself a suit of battle armor to protect his still-massive frame. Made of Asgardian steel, the armor was cast and constructed at a steel mill in Pittsburgh.

FIRST SEEN IN THOR #378, THOR LOST THIS GIANT SARDINE CAN IN A BATTLE WITH THE CELESTIALS IN THOR #389. HE THEN SHAVED HIS BEARD AND RESUMED HIS TRADITIONAL LOOK.

THUNDER

When the mortal but mighty Eric Masterson assumed the mantle of Thor, a battle with the troll Ulik left his traditional raiment in tatters. As handy with a needle as he was with a hammer, Masterson designed and tailored himself a somewhat updated outfit.

FIRST SEEN IN THOR #433, THIS UNIFORM WAS DISCARDED BY ERIC MASTERSON WHEN THE TRUE THOR RETURNED AND THE MORTAL DECIDED TO GO HIS OWN WAY AS THUNDERSTRIKE. ONCE AGAIN, THOR CLIMBED BACK INTO HIS OLD HOTPANTS AND TIGHTS.

MARVEL COMICS
THE 1ST ISSUE OF A STUNNING NEW EPIC!
THE MIGHTY THOR
THERE'S A NEW THUNDER GOD IN TOWN!!

A battle with the beastman Karnivor quickly shredded Thor's beloved traditional outfit. When Thor used his magic hammer, Mjolnir, to repair the damage, Mjolnir rearranged the molecules of the cloth into a new pattern... which, mercifully, was not paisley.

FIRST SEEN IN THOR #475, THOR WORE THIS UNIFORM WHILE ASSOCIATING WITH THE GODPACK.

But it wasn't to last. Once again, a fearsome battle took its toll on Thor's clothing. This time, perhaps under the influence of the Enchantress (who really knows how to dress), Thor went for the basic, barbaric look.

FIRST SEEN IN THOR #493, THIS OUTFIT'S MOST STRIKING FEATURE WAS THE FACT THAT IT LEFT OUR HERO NAKED FROM THE WAIST UP. YOWZA! WILL THE MIGHTY THOR RETAIN THIS OUTFIT AS BOTH WINTER AND ROB LIEFELD APPROACH? ONLY THE NORNS KNOW FOR SURE... AND THEY'RE NOT TELLING!

the FAMILY

BURI
Odin's Grandfather

MIMIR
Odin's Uncle

BORR
Odin's Father

VILI
Odin's Brother

HODER
God of Winter
Odin's Nephew

JORD
Earth Goddess

GRID
Storm Giantess

LAUFEY
Storm
Giant

FARBAUTI
Storm Giantess

LOKI
God of Evil
Odin's Adopted Son

THOR
God of Thunder

VIDAR
God of Strength

of ODIN

ODIN
All-Father
Lord of Asgard

VE
Odin's Brother

?

BESTLA
Giantess
Odin's Mother

FRIGGA
Goddess of Marriage

TYR
God of War

HERMOD
God of Speed

BALDER
God of Light

HOT FACTS about the HEAVY-HITTING

Thor's mighty hammer **Mjolnir** is one of the most awesome weapons ever wielded in the Marvel Universe!

The skull-cracker was lovingly crafted by a couple of enterprising dwarves named **Brokk** and **Eitri,** who chose a nearly indestructible metal called **Uru** for the project.

WHOSOEVER HOLDS THIS HAMMER, IF HE BE WORTHY, SHALL POSSESS THE POWER OF... THOR"

Later, Thor's dad **Odin** booted the hammer up with a bunch of enchantments. The first and foremost enchantment made it impossible for the hammer to be lifted by any living being unless he was worthy of it. This explains why the hammer has never been seen on "Wayne's World."

The second enchantment made the hammer always return to the hand that had thrown it, much like a boomerang or a stray cat.

The third enchantment enabled the weapon's owner to call down bolts of lightning, hurricane-force winds and driving rain at the drop of a hat (all right, at the stomp of the hammer).

IS HAMMER of THOR

The fourth, and possibly the "grooviest" enchantment made it possible for the hammer to create interspatial portals, which would allow travel into other dimensions, including Asgard.

IT IS TIME FOR MIGHTY THOR TO BECOME WEAK DOCTOR BLAKE AGAIN...

The fifth enchantment enabled Thor to assume his milk-toasty, mortal identity, with the rather obviously barbaric weapon turning into a gentlemanly cane. Of course, it helped if no one was looking!

The sixth enchantment turned the hammer into a private Learjet, figuratively speaking! All the mighty Thor had to do was toss the hammer in the air, grab hold of the leather thong wrapping the handle, and the thing would tow him all over Hel's half acre and beyond if he so desired.

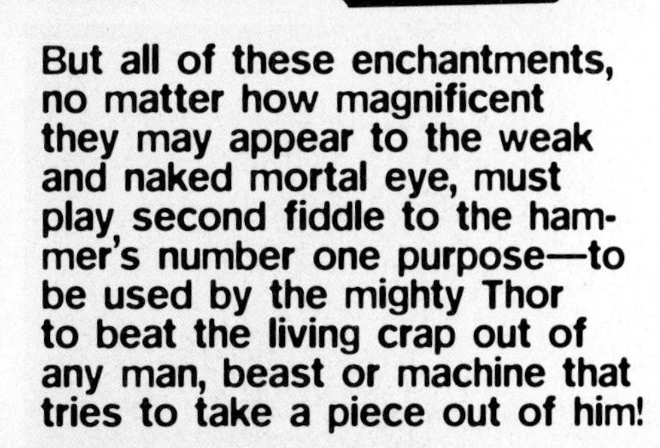

But all of these enchantments, no matter how magnificent they may appear to the weak and naked mortal eye, must play second fiddle to the hammer's number one purpose—to be used by the mighty Thor to beat the living crap out of any man, beast or machine that tries to take a piece out of him!

The first half of the book will be a smoking battlefield, courtesy of writer Bill Messner-Loebs and top artist Mike Deodato! After that, all h-e-double-hockeysticks breaks loose with a map of Asgard (Thor's homeland), a quiz that's stumped more than a few Marvel editors, and a dangerously informational article regarding the powers of Thor's hammer! Are you still standing? Good, because there's *MORE!!!!* There's gonna be a Thor quiz, a timeline chronicling the major events that have made up half a thousand issues of THOR, and strength comparison chart of Thor to his opponents! You'll get your money's worth on this one if you have to count out that $2.50 in *pennies!*

In case you have your doubts, though, Bill Messner-Loebs is more than happy to fill you in on the details. "Thor and the Enchantress are going to be sent to Asgard by Doctor Strange, only to find the place deserted by everyone they knew." The once-proud kingdom of Asgard is barren, and trolls and frost giants are fighting for the spoils. Thor and the Enchantress quickly go their separate ways, as Amora sides with the frost giants. Thor, much to his surprise, winds up fighting alongside a particularly large and ugly troll who was once his enemy.

“This should make (longtime *THOR* editor) Ralph Macchio very happy,”

chortles Messner-Loebs. “Ulik was the biggest and toughest troll in Asgard back in the Jack Kirby days—we're talking double-digit issues here. At one time, Ulik tried to prove that he was tougher than Thor. The dialogue in that issue borrowed heavily from Shakespeare; even Stan Lee couldn't keep a straight face at the end!”

Whether Messner-Loebs himself will borrow from the bard remains to be seen, but a sneak peek at the advance solicit sent out to retailers promised “hammer-through-the-helmet, ‘Braveheart’-type action.” Wow! It takes a special artist to show that kind of grisly carnage in a code-approved book, but Mike Deodato's more than up to the task! He could do it with boxing gloves on! But seriously, kids, the gloves are off for AVENGERS #400 and THOR #500, so if you like a good hard sock in the chops, there'll be two of them waiting for you at the comic shop this May!

—Polly Watson

The *Thor: The Legend* one-shot, published shortly after the series wrapped with #502, celebrated the title's decades-long history. Cover art by Mike Deodato Jr. & Marie Javins.

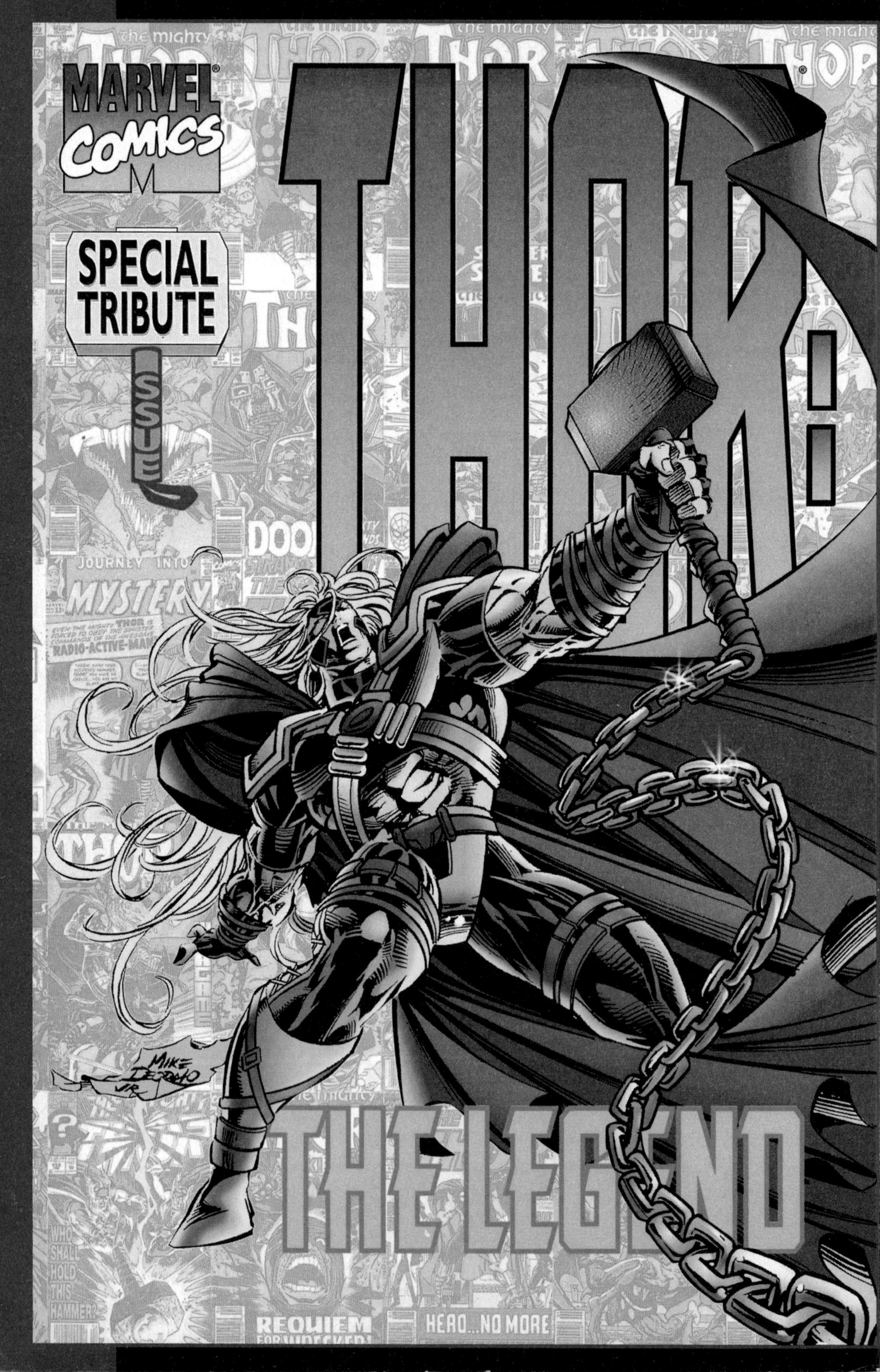